Malcolm Bird is the Developm~~~~~~~~~~~~~~~~~~~~~~
international insurance organisation centred in the City of
London.

He has over twenty years business experience in the UK and
overseas, with American and British companies. His work
has been in the fields of Organisation and Methods,
computers and general business consultancy.

A better way to manage

Malcolm Bird

SPHERE BOOKS LIMITED

SPHERE BOOKS LTD

Penguin Books Ltd, 27 Wrights Lane, London W8 5TZ (Publishing and Editorial)
and Harmondsworth, Middlesex, England (Distribution and Warehouse)
Viking Penguin Inc., 40 West 23rd Street, New York, New York 10010, USA
Penguin Books Australia Ltd, Ringwood, Victoria, Australia
Penguin Books Canada Ltd, 2801 John Street, Markham, Ontario, Canada L3R 1B4
Penguin Books (NZ) Ltd, 182–190 Wairau Road, Auckland 10, New Zealand

First published in Great Britain in 1985 by Duncan Publishing
Published by Sphere Books Ltd 1988

Printed and bound in Great Britain by
Richard Clay Ltd, Bungay, Suffolk

Contents

Introduction

Whatever problems exist in a company — falling sales, low morale, increasing costs, poor productivity — an investigator can frequently find common underlying causes: mistakes which are repeated over and over again. The author has observed these causes during many years in management, and this book is the result of an analysis of his notes.

Two main factors emerge from his work. First, a collection of attitudes — which are not unique to, but are particularly marked in, British management as opposed, say, to German, North American and French management. Second, that managers persistently repeat certain errors.

Learning how to manage successfully is neither quick nor easy. Many excellent books on management line the bookcases of executives, and training courses on many aspects of management are organised by reliable schools of management. But these demand concentration and effort — and a considerable amount of time. Moreover, some managers regard it as beneath their dignity to attend courses or say that the courses are not sufficiently pertinent. They acquire textbooks but give up reading beyond the first chapter — finding them hard-going or not relevant to their specific problems.

This, then, is a practical book designed to be enjoyable to read and to fill a gap in management literature. It covers what should be familiar ground and is based entirely on real life observation.

This approach, when related to the reader's real work situation, may arouse feelings of anguish, guilt or outrage. But it is hoped that, at least, this book will provoke thought and will stimulate managers to assess their own performance and to take specific positive steps to become more effective in their work.

1

Attitudes to employees

Team spirit and motivation

The administrator proudly conducted the VIP around a shiny new office building, anxious to show off the grand design. They eventually arrived at the staff canteen — a misnomer as, in fact, there were three separate eating areas. The first was a Self-service Cafeteria for junior staff, from where one could actually see the Managers' Restaurant with waitress service. Beyond was a fully enclosed Directors' Dining-room.

Not only had the company deliberately chosen to separate their employees when eating but also they had added some interesting refinements to underline status differences. The cafeteria had a tiled floor, while the other areas were carpeted. The managers received a free glass of red or white wine with their meals, while the directors could choose a free bottle of wine from a list.

Not only was this a more expensive construction job (a single restaurant would have been much cheaper) but the company had lost an opportunity to encourage a team-feeling between the employees of all levels. They had instead chosen to create or perpetuate a 'them and us' situation and instil an attitude which can be costly and damaging in any organisation. For instance, did the absence of a carpet in the cafeteria imply that the directors believed their subordinates to have such messy eating habits that a carpet would be ruined? Perhaps the absence of free wine might be construed as necessary to prevent irresponsible drinking,

1

even fighting, in the cafeteria? The managers, however, could be trusted with one glass of wine. Only directors could hold their liquor to the extent of a bottle!

Some typical justifications for this type of eating arrangement are:

- Seniors can discuss confidential matters, over lunch, when juniors are not present.
- We must maintain discipline and this is aided by status symbols.
- The arrangements will motivate people to strive for promotion.

Let us consider these more closely:

1. *The discussion of confidential matters:* This should take place in offices and conference rooms, undisturbed by considerations of the choice of food or wine and out of the earshot of waitresses. Thus this justification is little more than an excuse to avoid rubbing shoulders with juniors. For goodness sake, let managers admit this feeling and start from there.

2. *Discipline:* This is not maintained by status symbols. Such symbols are a subject of envy or derision among the 'have-nots' and become the cause of petty energy-consuming squabbles and manoeuvrings among the 'haves'. Discipline stems from respect and order and no manager should need the equivalent of a notice hanging around his neck saying 'I am important'. A good leader, with abilities to match his responsibility, will be respected by his subordinates. A poor manager will enhance the disrespect felt towards him if he shelters behind spurious symbols of importance.

3. *Motivation:* This comes from job satisfaction, a sense of participation and opportunities to be creative. Status separation can humiliate and make people feel uncomfortable or even angry. Such feelings demotivate.

Such 'justifications' then are mere excuses for a lack of confidence and misplaced feelings of superiority. Here in one new building of grand design was a lamentable absence of managerial know-how that could only damage the business.

Managers should never allow themselves to become out of touch with the shop-floor and should remember their own feelings when in a junior role. Staff at *all* levels need to be motivated. The means to do it have been clearly explained by such men as Herzberg, Maslow, Likert and MacGregor who have studied the subject and published the results. Their findings can be summarised in this way:

To make your employees *content* (not necessarily motivated) ensure that the following are right:

- Company policy and administration
- Personal relations
- Status (avoid humiliating divisions in the restaurant/canteen!)
- Salary
- Job security
- Social activity

To *motivate* employees provide one or more of the following:

- Interesting work — with challenge
- Scope for creativity
- Scope for, and a sense of, achievement
- Recognition of achievement
- Sense of responsibility (e.g. participation)
- Advancement and prospects

Management, at its peril, ignores the feelings of its staff far too often. Rensis Likert, in his book *The Human Organisation,* when talking about new systems said: 'The motivation of the members of an organisation can be crucial in determining whether labour-saving processes — computers or automated equipment — are made to work well or poorly. Supervisory and non-supervisory employees, if they wish to do so, can make excellent equipment perform unsatisfactorily and with frequent failures. These employees can also, if they desire to do so, rapidly eliminate the inadequacies in new processes or equipment and have the operation running smoothly in a surprisingly short time.'

Your staff are people too

Many systems and other business problems are rooted in discontent among staff generated by supposedly intelligent, mature managers who have no idea how to keep their people happy. They fail to treat their staff like people — human beings with feelings, fears and hopes. Simple courtesy will take a manager a long way. Notice how the successful manager takes a real interest in his employees' work and problems; he offers help and gives it. He treats subordinates as colleagues rather than inferiors.

Management, at its peril, ignores the feelings of its staff.

One administrative manager was given the task of improving the performance of a filing service of about 20 people. 'They were a bloody-minded and unenthusiastic bunch with a marked couldn't-care-less attitude,' he remarked. He found that they suffered from having had:

—no particular boss to report to;
—grossly inadequate training;
—no clear instructions;
—low status — everyone else in the company treated them as dog's-bodies.

There were other problems, all of which had been clearly caused by the company's management attitudes. Generally, the management were convinced that the filing clerks were stupid, lazy and generally useless. However, after a few months' hard work, the situation improved substantially. The whole problem was neatly summed up by this rather sad comment to the administration manager made by one of the clerks: 'I feel much happier now. You know, no one took any interest in me before.'

Whether or not the management in this case cared at all about these people, one thing is certain: the poor filing service hindered management, wasted money and reduced profits. There need be no conflict between profit and the proper treatment of people.

Action check list

☐ Look after your human assets
  —Keep in touch
  —Find ways to motivate.

☐ Avoid damaging status differences.

☐ Protect your human investment: recruitment and training costs money — don't waste it.

2

Training, development and delegation

'It took me 25 years to learn this job and young Snooks expects to be promoted after only 5 years . . . wet behind the ears . . . impatient . . . lacks experience . . .' Thus speaks the so-called manager who cannot cope with youthful ambition.

If it takes a person 25 years to learn *any* job then that person must be a very slow learner indeed! If his predecessor also took 25 years then some interesting arithmetic emerges. Assuming a person has 45 years' working life of which 25 years are taken up learning the job, then his successor must start learning before the person himself has finished learning — or there will be no one to look after the shop! This attitude to learning is as foolish as the statement that you cannot train managers, they are born.

The 'management-training-is-bunk' school

Some of the worst managers would describe themselves as 'natural' managers. They are part of the 'management-training-is-bunk' school of thought — ignorant of their own ignorance. It is not hard for the O & M man to find cases of poor performance due largely to managers who refuse to train or develop their staff, and will not delegate. Their departments are inefficient and regarded as such, but their own arrogance and complacency shield them from the fact. The following example, which occurred in a small North American company, illustrates this situation.

The managing director was a hard-working and technically able man. He was supported by four immediate subordinates, all of whom were overworked and depressed. At the next level down were some 20 quite demoralised youngsters with good qualifications but little to do. The performance of the company was mediocre.

An O & M survey found that the basic problem was the managing director himself, who worked on the principle that he should make all commercial decisions. His immediate subordinates thus had no real authority and were often working their heads off keeping a situation going until the MD had time to make a decision.

After all the staff from MD to office boy had been interviewed, a draft report was prepared for discussion with the MD. The crux of the recommendations was to start a training programme for:

— the junior staff to equip them for delegated work,
— the four senior men to be involved in decision making; and,
— delegating authority to the four men.

The objective was to utilise to the full all the labour and skills available to eliminate backlogs of work, to provide improved services to customers, to reduce errors (tired men make more mistakes), to prepare people as successors for the future, and to improve morale.

The MD was wholly opposed and the nature of this response was not uncommon. His arguments went like this:

1. We have no time to train.
2. I cannot depend on my subordinates to make the right decisions.
3. Many of the staff are lazy.
4. Many of the staff lack the necessary intelligence.
5. Why should the youngsters be 'pushed along' — I had to serve an apprenticeship of 20 years.

The fact is that if a manager has no time to train his staff, he has no time for the future of the company. It is the younger people who are the future of the company, not the older ones with retirement in sight.

Mediocrity is self-generating

The excuse that a manager cannot depend on his subordinates is a weak cover-up for bad management. It is part of the manager's job to select staff and teach them. If they are inadequate, he may need to sack them. The same applies to staff that are lazy — though, in practice, there are few truly lazy people. There are, however, many demotivated people, without a real job to do and ignored by their managers.

The manager is himself responsible for:

— recruiting
— designing and defining work to be done
— teaching the people how to do the work
— giving them the chance to do it.

The MD in the illustration above had to hear the facts: 'You recruited the people and if they are no good for the job then the fault is yours. If they are lazy, lacking in knowledge or demotivated, what are you doing about it? The responsibility is yours. The solutions lie in your hands.'

Some managers lack the confidence to develop their staff and encourage good people because they see them as a threat to their own jobs. Thus the mediocre boss encourages mediocrity. Mediocrity quickly becomes self-generating. Managers, in their own interest, should encourage their staff to develop for the following reasons:

1. The department will perform better and this enhances the manager's own reputation.
2. Trained successors make it easier for the manager to be promoted. (The converse is also true.)
3. Successful training and delegation reduces pressure on the manager.

There are many good sources of information on how to train and delegate. Managers should study them. In the meantime, at all costs, avoid saying:

'I have no reliable staff.'
'I have no time to teach.'
'I can do it faster myself.'
'I agree in principle but . . .'
'We will do this when things are less busy.'

One more comment is needed on training, or the lack of it. Consider how often an employee is promoted to a new management job and only then trained how to manage, if trained at all. All staff taking, or likely to take, a management job should be trained well in advance. Long service and technical knowledge are not enough.

Action check list

Do . . .

☐ Take every opportunity to study training methods.

☐ Train junior staff to carry out delegated tasks reliably.

☐ Involve staff in decision making.

☐ Build up a training programme to prepare senior people as successors for the future.

Don't . . .

☐ . . . delegate work and forget it. Some help may be needed by the subordinate.

☐ . . . delegate and then interfere every five minutes. This is the same as saying 'I don't trust you, young Jenkins'.

☐ . . . delegate and then create hell over every mistake made. Has anyone learned a job without making a mistake here and there?

Attitudes to new recruits

Many organisations discover that a high turnover of staff occurs within the first six months of their recruitment. In other words, a significant proportion of bright-eyed enthusiasts who join companies (there is usually some enthusiasm at the start!) become so disenchanted that they leave after only a few weeks or months. This costs the company money, disrupts work and represents a significant amount of human misery. Why does it happen? Frequently because the new recruit is given no proper induction into the company.

'We'd like to offer you the job . . .'

Three real life cases illustrate just about all the classic errors:

New boy Alan

Alan, a 30-year old systems analyst with a successful career to date, arrived for his first day at his new company. He found that no one knew he was coming, there was no provision for a desk or chair and the boss was out for the day!

He waited around in reception for about two hours and the receptionist showed her irritation at his presence. Eventually someone conducted him to an unoccupied office where he sat, alone, until lunchtime. After lunch he asked his boss's secretary whether he should meet anyone or if there was any work for him. She, embarrassed, introduced him to another analyst who proceeded to tell him what a lousy company he had joined.

The second day was much the same — the boss to whom he had been told to report was still out and no one else showed any interest in him. His boss appeared on the third day and finally found time to speak to him about 11.00 am. The welcome from the boss comprised a few remarks to the effect that he understood that he now had an office and seemed to be sorted out. Alan's request for a specific job to do, however, was fobbed off. New boy Alan twiddled his thumbs, virtually ignored, for the rest of the day. On day four, he resigned.

New boy Bob

Bob, a 17-year-old, joined a bank on the first day of his first job. He was welcomed by the manager and handed over to Mrs Fogey who was retiring in two weeks' time. Mrs Fogey had the task of teaching him how to operate

Somewhat bewildered and scared, Bob tried his best to work out what to do.

a computer terminal, and yet the instructions lasted for just 15 minutes. They went like this:

'You switch on here and watch the green light. Sort your 456s into piles by account number order and punch the key code first. Then avoid any contra items which, by rights, should be dealt with as a 209. By the way, 209s should all be debit items unless there is a transfer involved in which case you use a pink docket . . .'

At the end of the instruction period, Mrs Fogey left Bob to do the job. Somewhat bewildered and scared, he tried his best to work out what to do but made a hopeless mess of the job. At the end of the day he was told by a passing manager: *'Never never* do something you are unsure about. Refer to Mrs Fogey and she will help you.' Fine advice!

During the second and third days Bob sought help from Mrs Fogey but she was always too busy and rather unfriendly.

Bob was keen to please and tenacious too. He began to build up notes on what to do (that is, to assemble a procedure manual) and, in the evenings, he obtained explanations from his father regarding such mysterious terms as credit, debit and transfer. Despite his care he continued to make mistakes and received criticism (but no help) from the deputy manager. Finally, in desperation, he asked to see the manager. The manager referred him back to the deputy manager. The deputy manager marked him down as a trouble-maker, told him he was not very bright and gave him 'his last chance'.

With help from his father Bob continued to try to learn by trial and error but, because he received no help or encouragement at work, decided to leave after just six months in the job.

New girl Flora

Flora, a middle-aged married lady returning to work after raising a family, reported at a branch of a financial institution on her first day. The branch receptionist had no record of her and Flora was told: 'Sorry, it must be a mistake; I'd better direct you to our other branch.' The second branch referred her back to the first which, after some persistence, Flora found was to be her place of work. She was collected from reception by her boss who made some tactless remarks about her being late on the first day.

Flora was given some work to do and introduced to her colleagues. At lunchtime everyone else disappeared and she found a nearby sandwich bar. Not sure how long she had for lunch she hurried back. Her colleagues eventually returned and she discovered that they had been to the company's staff canteen.

During her second day she found the canteen and lunched alone. It became quickly apparent that, as she was middle-aged, her colleagues, with an average age of about 20, wanted nothing to do with her. The days went by, she did her work, but felt ever more lonely. Attempts at friendly conversations were snubbed and she was consistently ignored by her boss.

After a few weeks Flora decided to leave. When she handed in her resignation to her boss he said: 'Just as well; I don't think you fitted in here.'

Preparing to welcome new recruits

What should we learn from all this? As a manager you should try to answer the following questions:

1. Do you remember your first few days in a new job? How did you feel?
2. Did you experience any of the following:
   — a feeling of loneliness?
   — a feeling of not belonging?
   — fear?
   — uncertainty about what you should be doing?
   — not knowing who was who?
   — not knowing who was your boss?
   — not knowing where to find things/people?
   — not knowing what other people did?
   — not knowing the purpose of your work?
   — not knowing how to do your job?
   — not knowing the company rules, even the working hours?
   — not understanding the jargon?

3. Did you feel:
   — discouraged?
   — ready to walk out?
   — sorry you had changed jobs?
   — angry about the way you were treated?
   — misled at your interview?
   — a feeling of inferiority?
   — confused?
   — overawed by others?

If you answered yes to *any* of these questions then someone failed to welcome you and introduce you to your new job in the right way. What a manager should do about new employees is really common sense.

Action check list

☐ Make the new employee feel welcome; give your receptionist his or her name.

☐ Introduce the employee to others.

☐ Give the newcomer a *worthwhile* job to do.

☐ Explain carefully:
  — the job to be done
  — what is expected of the new employee
  — *how* to do the job
  — when, where to do the job
  — the purpose of the job
  — the standards required

☐ Provide the necessary tools of the trade — forms, books, machinery, etc. — and make certain that they are all in working order, clean and tidy.

☐ Appoint a 'buddy' to help out over the first few days.

☐ Explain all the important company rules, and why they exist.

☐ Offer help if needed, and give it when asked for. Be patient with the newcomer's difficulties.

☐ Above all, be friendly. Show pleasure that the newcomer has started. After all, you should be pleased. You have probably been fighting tooth and nail for a long time to obtain an additional person.

Attitudes to planning and achievement

'What do we want to achieve and how do we do it?'

Many failures are founded on lack of a target coupled, inevitably, with a lack of a plan. The failing manager has no target to aim at and no plan. He may say that he is too busy coping with all the day-to-day problems; or he may be opposed to planning on the grounds that it is impossible to foretell the future, and he can deal with tomorrow's problems tomorrow. This is really to say that he is drifting along with the tide and hoping for the best.

One typical opponent of planning was an insurance underwriter. Nevertheless, while opposed to planning for financial matters, marketing, manpower, and so on, he did insure his own house in case it burnt down; yet he was not prepared to think ahead in business. He failed to see that his own job as an underwriter existed only because other people planned ahead. Such attitudes are at the root of many failures and disappointments.

So, starting at the top, the company must clarify its objectives and state its policy. It is desirable to have a considered view on all the basic subjects, for example:

- What business are we in?
- Where and with whom do we do business?
- What size business do we aim for?
- What market share do we want? . . . and so on.

Such attitudes are at the root of many failures and disappointments.

Managers may regard the answers as self-evident ('Everyone knows what business we are in') and the questions unnecessary. But this reaction changes when the managers are made to sit down and work out the answers. They may find, for example, that although the company has been making and selling shirts for 10 years the simple statement that 'shirt-making (and selling) is the business' may not be sufficient. The manager who answers, for example, 'men's clothing', obviously has a different outlook and is likely to have the vision to open up a whole new world of business for the company. Twenty years ago Marks & Spencer might have been described as being in the clothing business. Today, M & S sell books, flowers and food. The company now can be described as being in the retail sales business. Today, Boots the chemist also sell television sets, luggage, crockery, stationery, etc. Boots, too, are now in the retail sales business. If these companies had stuck to their original lines of business only, they would doubtless be much smaller, less secure and probably less profitable than they are today.

Not every businessman wants his company to grow as large as Marks & Spencer or Boots, but he should encourage his managers to work out the growth the company *wants* to achieve. Much growth occurs by accident, resulting in financial problems and disorder. Failure to grow can cause a string of problems too, and management must carefully calculate what is likely to be best for the company and its employees. Redundancy is often a result of management's failure to plan ahead, and when redundancy is used as an expedient measure by management it is a crime against the victims, and may incite the worst elements in the trade unions.

Define objectives in measurable terms

Once management has worked out the basic philosophy (which will need to be regularly reviewed), objectives should be laid down. An easy way to set objectives is to choose ones which cannot be measured. The manager who chooses the objective 'To improve customer service' is ducking the issue. What does this really mean? And what will his staff make of it? To make the objective meaningful it should be defined in measurable terms, thus:

'To improve customer service by meeting all orders within 5 working days, reducing invoicing errors by 50% and answering all customer queries within 48 hours. These targets to be achieved by January 1st.'
With an objective like this, the manager and his staff have something

understandable to aim for, and they can work out how to achieve the targets.

Adjusting to changing circumstances

Managers often complain that they have no time for planning. This is really another case of having no time for the future of the organisation and its staff. The manager's role, inescapably, *is* to be concerned with

A common failing of companies is to ignore suggestions or plans drawn up by a younger person, just because he is younger.

the future, and the more senior the manager the further ahead he should be looking. The really successful top businessmen have one thing in common: vision. Failure to look ahead may result from complacency or, just as bad, apathy . . .

One hundred and fifty years ago there was a thriving company named Watkinson's Wicks, serving the candlemaking industry. The founder, Josiah Watkinson, had been in business for 30 years when his son, young Edward, expressed interest in and some concern about the up and coming gas lighting industry.

'Father,' said Edward, 'perhaps we should consider making gas mantles?'

'What!' bellowed old Josiah. 'That new fangled gas nonsense will never work, and I'll have nowt to do with it.'

Twenty years later, the demand for candles had fallen. Watkinson's Wicks finally folded up, and old Josiah died a sad and puzzled man. Young Mr Edward, who had faithfully followed his father's advice to save two pence a week, found that he had just enough capital to start a new company — Modern Gas Mantles — in the premises formerly occupied by Watkinson's Wicks. Edward's business thrived. Thirty years later, Mr Edward Watkinson, prosperous and content, was approached by his son, Nigel.

'Father,' said young Nigel, 'have you ever thought of making electric light bulbs? This new lighting by electricity could be a thing of the future.'

'Never!' said old Edward. 'Stick with the business you know, my boy. Besides, electricity will never catch on, you mark my words. It's unnatural and no one will ever find the capital to lay wires across the country — let alone build power stations.'

Twenty years later, old Edward died, a sad and bewildered bankrupt. Nigel, having seen both his grandfather and father ruined by their businesses, decided that starting up a company is too risky and so he became a milkman.

The moral of this story for managers is don't ignore or dismiss plans which have been drawn up by a younger person, just because he is younger. A common failing of companies is to place certain planning responsibilities with a young executive and then pull his ideas to pieces as soon as he presents anything a little unusual.

The younger managers and staff are more able to adjust to changing circumstances and are ready to think about new ideas and how to implement them. They should be encouraged. Planning ahead has the merit not only of aiding the business in adjusting to changing circumstances but also in ensuring that there is a regular re-think of objectives and actions.

Inevitably, planning must lead to change and this, as the next chapter tells, presents another set of problems.

Action check list

☐ Know (or demand to know) your company's objectives and policy.

☐ Make time for planning ahead, and do it regularly.

☐ Involve your staff in establishing your company's/department's objectives and policy.

☐ Make sure all your staff know and understand the policy and what *measurable* objectives have been set. (If you have involved your staff in the choice, they will be far more receptive and committed to achieving the targets set.)

☐ Listen carefully to the views of younger staff: one or two of them might have the 'vision' needed to open up a whole new world of business for your company.

5

The problems of change

Machiavelli, in his book *The Prince,* wrote: 'There is nothing more difficult to carry out, nor more doubtful of success, nor more dangerous to handle, than to initiate a new order of things. For the reformer has enemies in all those who profit by the old order, and only lukewarm defenders in all those who would profit by the new order, this lukewarmness arising partly from fear of their adversaries — and partly from the incredulity of mankind, who do not truly believe in anything new until they have had actual experience of it.'

Although this was written in the sixteenth century, people have not altered much in the intervening years. No manager can afford to give way to the human reluctance to consider change. But it should never be change for the sake of it. Managers must develop the mental discipline necessary to realise that the world will not stand still to please them and, like it or not, they must be constantly ready and willing to change when change is desirable or necessary. No organisation on its own can control the environment in which it operates, and it will suffer the consequences of every failure to react to circumstances.

External influences

Every business is subject to some or all of the following uncontrollable external influences:

- Rates of exchange
- Rates of interest
- Tax legislation
- Action of competitors
- Levels of world trade
- Commodity prices
- Public taste and fashions
- Wars — and other lunatic actions of politicians
- New technology

These external forces will vary and there is absolutely nothing a manager can do about them — except to plan ahead, forecasting events as intelligently as he can and *changing his own activities* to suit. The manager who is doggedly opposed to change will suffer the buffeting of external forces and, Canute-like, will get his shoes and socks wet.

This real-life case illustrates the ridiculous behaviour of some managements and unions in spite of being faced with a changing market environment and stronger competition.

Production was low at the Grappler New Era factory — despite modern machinery — and the company was making a loss on the product concerned. The main cause of the problem was a hold-up in production created whenever a minor, unskilled adjustment was needed on a machine. These adjustments were regularly required and took about a minute to accomplish.

The unions had traditionally insisted that adjustments were fitters' work and should not be carried out by a machine operator. Fitters were in short supply and machines could be out of action for any time between one and four hours until a fitter was available.

The union representative was asked if he would agree to operators doing the work and gave a horrified refusal. It was pointed out that the company was making a loss on the product and if things did not improve there was a danger that the factory would be closed down. This, of course, meant redundancy for all the union members.

The union representative was unimpressed. He maintained that the management was lying since, if the company made a loss on the product, management would not wish to increase production — thus increasing the size of the loss!

An Administration Manager suggested to him that if he would not take management's word for it he would arrange for the books of account to be made available to a union-appointed accountant who could tell him the financial facts. The union man said he would think about it. In the meantime the Administration Manager explained the idea to the Production Director who was aghast because, as he put it, 'It is contrary to our policy to allow such confidential information to be seen by outsiders'.

Neither of these men would compromise and eventually production was transferred to a continental factory where the unions and management were more flexible.

When Britain still had a sizeable motorcycle industry an African who had just purchased a Japanese motorcycle commented: 'I know it may not be as reliable as a British machine but the Japanese offer more colours and the bikes are more pretty.' No doubt the British management and unions in the motorcycle factories would have sneered at this attitude, but where are they now?

Action check list

☐ Consider the changes that are likely to affect the industry you are working in over the next few years.

☐ Write down your plans for coping with the changes, and for taking advantage of new opportunities.

☐ Ensure that you are preparing your staff for necessary and foreseeable changes.

Attitudes to business techniques

The expression 'business techniques' refers to a range of tools of the management trade including such methods as:

Inventory control	Marketing research
Appraisal schemes	Decision tree analysis
Manpower planning	Corporate planning
Operations research techniques	Production planning

A significant percentage of managers is opposed to using business techniques — although it seems that many detractors have no real idea what the techniques are or what they involve.

The anti-technique brigade tends to disguise unwillingness, ignorance and complacency behind expressions like: 'We in this organisation are different from anybody else and therefore these techniques do not apply to us.' The corollary, of course, is: 'I am not prepared to consider whether these techniques will help me, my staff, my bosses or the business, and the easiest reaction for me is to say that we are different.'

'That would never work here'

The manager should avoid saying that the technique concerned is not applicable until he is absolutely sure that this is the case; and certainly not without having ascertained what the technique is or involves.

Such a case occurred at Boondocks Engineering Co. where a thorny problem was being discussed. Someone present at the meeting put forward a potential solution involving the application of a particular type of equipment and a particular technique for using it. Another person present, without any hesitation, stated 'That would never work here'.

At a later stage the objector admitted that his objection had no foundation: he was unfamiliar with the nature of the proposal being put forward, had never seen the equipment suggested and had no idea whether in fact it would work. He similarly had no knowledge of the philosophy or technique that was implied.

Some months later the suggested solution was applied and it worked extremely well.

It has been demonstrated many times that the selection and correct application of an appropriate technique can be extremely valuable in furthering the aims of the business. It is important, of course, that the techniques are selected by someone who is expert not only in the techniques but also in the aspect of business under consideration, and that application is similarly monitored by an informed person.

Whilst a good manager will make an effort to discover and learn the techniques appropriate to his particular job or business, he will also carefully avoid abdicating his management responsibilities to the specialist who may be called upon to help him. The manager must remain in charge.

Advantages of the right technique

Without using some sort of technique, management tends to be based on expediency — leaping from one panic to another as crisis follows crisis and priority piles itself on priority.

Three real life instances demonstrate the potential advantages of applying the right technique.

Case 1

The manager of a warehouse was having considerable difficulty with stocktaking which was giving rise to excessive amounts of overtime which he could ill afford.

The manager was persuaded to permit an analysis of movements into and out of the warehouse to take place and certain statistical tests to be carried out. These showed conclusively that approximately 12 per cent of all the stocktaking work was entirely unnecessary and, having removed it, the overtime problem disappeared.

Case 2

The accountants constantly complained that an engineering stores was perpetually over-stocked, which was costly for the company. The store-keeper, always afraid of a stock-out position which would call down upon his head the wrath of the engineering department, strove to maintain maximum stocks.

A visual stock control system was introduced combined with application of an economic order quantity approach, with orders being placed according to a calculated re-order point schedule. The store-keeper found, rather to his surprise, that he could safely reduce the quantities held on the shelves without endangering his ability to meet requirements. The accountants were duly satisfied with the reduction in cash tied up, and the situation was further rationalised at a later stage by the application of Pareto's principle. (This interesting and simple 'technique' is outlined in British Institute of Management 'Guidelines for the Smaller Business' no. 14.)

Case 3

An estimating department staffed with well-experienced people was becoming more and more behind in its work to the point where orders which depended on their estimates were being endangered.

The customary reflex action of asking for more staff had emerged but, as suitable people were difficult to obtain, a study of the department was

It is also sensible to make the time we spend at work as enjoyable as possible.

made. Activity sampling applied to the work of the department showed that although the number of estimates required to be done and their general complexity had not altered over the years, there had been a transfer of other work into the department of which no one was consciously aware.

Rearrangement of the work in accordance with the activity sampling results removed the problem completely and avoided the necessity of taking on more people.

There is one other important, though less obvious, incentive for managers to use the various techniques available: it is that they make life rather more interesting. Whether we like it or not, we have to spend eight or more hours a day at work and it is therefore sensible to make that period of time as enjoyable as possible.

Action check list

☐ Don't dismiss business techniques as irrelevant.

☐ Find out what they are and how they might help you. This is part of a manager's responsibilities to the business.

☐ Make a point of learning techniques yourself — at least to a level where you are not blindly in the hands of a specialist.

7

Management and the facts

It is the responsibility of managers to make decisions and these decisions should be based on facts. This is far from always being the case, and one of the most common faults is to make decisions based on emotions, guesses, hunches or damn-all.

'It is a well-known fact . . .'

At a meeting where marketing decisions were being discussed, someone voiced the view that the time was right to push for a larger share of the market. This view was certainly correct in terms of the need to increase revenue, since costs had been steadily rising for a considerable time whilst income was virtually stagnant.

One of the participants was strongly opposed to the idea of striving for a larger market share on the grounds that if a larger share was obtained it would attract unwelcome attention and be politically undesirable. He based this view on a positive statement that the company already had 33 per cent of the market.

When challenged on this fairly precise assessment of market share he stated that it was a 'well-known fact'. Fortunately the real figures were immediately to hand and showed quite clearly that the market share was closer to 25 per cent. With the view that an excess above 33 per cent was politically dangèrous then the company still had plenty more spare capacity to develop.

Managers should avoid at all costs acting on the 'well-known fact'. The statement that something is a well-known fact frequently signifies that the author of the statement would like it to be true or finds it convenient to say so at the time, but has no evidence whatsoever to back it up.

Among the well-known facts heard at meetings are the following:

- *It is cheaper to print stationery externally.* In fact, it proved to be about double the cost of internal printing.
- *Only about one per cent of United Kingdom companies carry out corporate planning.* This statement was made in 1976. The Institute of Personnel Management reported, in 1975, the results of a survey which found that around 80 per cent of a sample of 308 companies of all sizes in the United Kingdom used corporate planning. This evidence, even if based on a relatively small sample, indicated that the number of companies involved in corporate planning was very much greater than the one per cent stated.
- *Clients of the firm will not accept an increase in fees and it will be extremely dangerous to try this on.* This statement was made despite the fact that the firm concerned had been making a loss for some considerable time. When an increase in fees was put to clients it was accepted with very little resistance indeed.
- *There will be a problem of shortage of staff in the town being considered for company re-location, as it is a well-known fact that there is competition for staff in the area.* Enquiries showed that, at the time the statement was made, there were more than 400 suitably qualified people on the professional and executive register and many thousands on the ordinary roll of job-seekers at the local job centre.

Many decisions are based entirely on opinion when it would not have been difficult to ascertain the truth. For example, opinions have been quoted on the capacity of machinery when a quick 'phone call to the suppliers would confirm what the capacity really was. Even worse are decisions based on someone's guess (unqualified) as to what the law states on a particular point. It is not difficult to telephone a solicitor to find out the facts or even to buy a book on the relevant law.

The problem is that hard facts can only be ascertained by enquiry which takes time and means that an effort has to be made. However, it does mean that better decisions are likely to be taken and sometimes that decisions are easier to take: it is not unusual for the facts, when discovered, to point clearly to the decision needed thus relieving management of the burden of agonising for hours over something about which they are uncertain.

Without facts, managers agonise for hours and make decisions based on emotions, guesses, hunches or damn-all.

The obstacles game

Looking for the obstacles is a game played by a wide variety of executives. Perhaps it is popular because it is extremely easy to play.

> At some point in the early stages of the war (it is reported), Winston Churchill was approached by one of his ministers responsible for the production of war materials. The minister enumerated at length the difficulties which he faced.
>
> Churchill replied: 'Mr X, you have now successfully entrenched yourself behind your difficulties — please explain to me how you plan to overcome them.'

In the above story the game player was motivated by a feeling of sorrow for himself whereas in most business cases the players are motivated by a need to show how alert and knowledgeable they are at meetings!

The rules of the game are very simple. One participant at a meeting puts forward an idea or proposal for consideration. The game players then immediately begin to outline all the difficulties that they can foresee. This is usually carried out at a considerable speed because none of the participants takes any trouble to think about the proposal in any way or gives the proposer the opportunity to bring forward any of the basic facts on which his proposal is based (if he has any).

> During a meeting at the Tipple Drinks Co. a proposal was put forward for a staff restaurant to be installed in a particular building — this proposal being made after considerable enquiry and a lot of fact gathering.
>
> A master of the art of playing the game immediately responded by bringing forward twenty different obstacles in the space of some five minutes. He was unaware that a report with facts and figures was available and this encouraged him in a masterly performance of displaying his mental agility. He started off by agreeing to the idea in principle and then immediately stated the following objections amongst others:
>
> (a) Outsiders will use the restaurant and it will be swamped with people from adjacent premises.
> (b) A very costly subsidy will be required.
> (c) It will be difficult to hire the necessary catering staff.
> (d) There will be a lot of wasted food.
> (e) There was a luncheon voucher scheme already in existence.
> (f) There will be a lot of washing-up to be done.

Having put forward twenty different obstacles in the space of some five minutes, the game player rested back in his seat with a smug smile of satisfaction.

(g) The staff will want to have alcohol served and this would not be acceptable.

(h) There will be no suitable place to put the staff restaurant in the building.

Having fired these shots with amazing rapidity, the game player rested back in his seat with a smug smile of satisfaction.

Fortunately, all the objections had been anticipated when the preliminary enquiries were made, and they were satisfactorily dealt with. Eventually Tipple did install a staff canteen which was a great success.

However, the snag with the obstacle game is that it wastes time. It can also create bad feeling because raising obstacles implies that the person making the proposal has not been astute enough to consider all the difficulties himself, and that he requires the brilliance of the game player to point out the obvious. This causes stress between individuals and encourages others to join in the game at a later stage in situations where they feel they can get their revenge.

It also represents another serious problem in that many people, when faced with a new idea, are worried by it and are easily influenced by objections made by others. They may cling to real or imagined difficulties as a means to avoid tackling a seemingly difficult problem.

It is akin to the situation in a court of law where the lawyer, having made some quite unacceptable statement about the accused or a witness, is pulled up by the judge who instructs the jury to disregard the comment made. But having heard the comment, it is impossible for anyone to disregard it totally however objective he may be. Thus, at meetings, the man who produces a whole string of objections, complaints or whatever is stirring up the fears of others and making it far more difficult for them to think objectively about the facts and figures presented.

Action check list

☐ Before making a decision on the basis of 'hunch' or 'gut feeling', seek relevant *facts*.

☐ Beware of being put off a course of action by objections based on hunch or gut feeling. Check the validity of the objections first.

Born leaders

A young business studies graduate on a preliminary management training course was at one stage in his programme placed in a department run by a man called Gerald, who was well-known for being not only a martinet but thoroughly disagreeable, bad-tempered and rude to his staff. Gerald had a large department ranging from junior clerks to quite senior grade managers, and his attitude had for some time been a cause of concern to his superiors.

The management trainee had spent about a month in this department when at a routine review session with his training guide he mentioned that Gerald had been on a Man Management course. He was asked what difference the course had made to Gerald's attitude.

'Well,' said the management trainee, 'prior to going on the course, it was Gerald's habit to come into the office at 9 o'clock in the morning, walk round, scowl at everybody, say nothing and walk out. Since the course, he comes into the office at 9 o'clock every morning, walks round, smiles at everybody, says nothing and walks out!'

Undoubtedly Gerald was one of those people to whom simple courtesy and an understanding nature did not come easily. At some point in the course, he must have been told: whatever you do, be nice to people, smile at them — and he thought he was following this out carefully; but his heart was by no means in it. In other words, Gerald found it impossible to change his basic nature; and the cynicism with which he was treated by his staff reflected the fact that they recognised this.

Managers of this sort tend to cause damage to the organisation simply because their staff do not respect them, cannot admire them, and are not motivated by them.

A selection of damaging manager types

Perhaps the reader may have come across some of these categories of manager who have a damaging effect on their departments?

1. The Nervous Manager

This is the man — often promoted too quickly — who is unable to make any decisions; on the rare occasions when he does manage to make a decision he will change his mind ten minutes later. In other words, he lacks confidence in his own actions, and is anxious about the reactions of his bosses and even possibly of his subordinates. As a result his staff become frustrated and uncertain as to what is likely to happen, and the best of them soon begin to look around for a job elsewhere.

2. The Tycoon

This one feels that he must demonstrate his seniority by shouting, and by refusing to listen to his subordinates. He is likely to boast in the pub around the corner about firing people. He is prone to dramatic gestures such as thumping his desk and reducing his secretary to tears. He is probably nagged by his wife. And, as a colleague once remarked to me, he nearly always seems to wear a moustache and suede boots!

Younger staff seem to be terrified of people like this and as a consequence direct their efforts into avoiding his notice. Older staff who have remained with him tend to be sycophantic toadies or bored no-hopers.

3. The Creep

This is the man who lacks conviction and spends his time being sycophantic to his own bosses to the detriment of his own staff.

A real-life example from this category insisted that one of his subordinates did a job in a certain way and refused to listen to the reasonable protests that his subordinate put forward. At a subsequent meeting with the director of the department, the work of the subordinate was severely criticised and the creep manager turned round to this unfortunate person and said 'Paul, I told you not to do it that way'. Paul was astonished and deeply hurt by this unjust blame from the creep boss who clearly was prepared to damage anyone else's reputation in order to preserve his own.

4. The 'Reggie Perrin'

This man has become thoroughly tired, cynical and bored.

Whilst he may be wrestling with a chip on his shoulder (perhaps overlooked for promotion in the past) he has the unfortunate habit of making his staff approach their work with the same lack of interest and enthusiasm as himself.

5. The Genius Monopolist

This one knows it all and under no circumstances is he prepared to obtain the views of his staff on a particular question or to discuss any problems with them.

He normally talks to his staff only to issue instructions and will brook no argument on any matter. He likes to use expressions such as 'You are not paid to think'. One can only conclude that the man who prefers staff not to think would be happier using computers to do all the work since these are machines which cannot think and are at all times totally obedient.

Developing the constructive approach

It is, however, more constructive to consider those attributes of leaders who have a tendency to promote success in their departments. A thorough scrutiny of the techniques of successful managers over a number of years has revealed the presence of the following features:

(a) The staff have no inhibitions in discussing their work with the boss and certainly are not afraid of him.

(b) Whenever a problem has to be solved, the boss is willing and anxious to obtain his subordinates' ideas as to solutions.

(c) The staff are motivated not by fear or threats, but by some form of reward which, to be most effective, is linked with achievement of objectives previously agreed by all concerned.

(d) The manager himself is not the only one who feels responsible for achieving objectives since he has successfully encouraged this feeling in all of his staff.

(e) A great deal of communication (often informal and ad hoc) goes on and there are explanations of and discussions concerning circumstances, requirements and so on within the department.

(f) Allied to (e) above, information flows freely in all directions and is positively encouraged by the manager to flow upwards.

(g) Any information given to the subordinates by the boss is freely and openly discussed in the presence of the manager thus removing the suspicion that often accompanies information flowing downwards.

(h) The manager makes it abundantly clear that he wants to hear bad news as well as good, and does everything he can to encourage an upward flow of information which is accurate, complete and factual.

(i) The manager has considerable knowledge of the problems of his subordinates and in addition to this knowledge makes a serious attempt to understand the problems and to understand the feelings of those dealing with them.

(j) Team work is encouraged at all levels even to the extent that the manager is prepared to place himself in a team working on a particular project or problem of which one of his subordinates is, temporarily at least, the leader.

(k) Whilst the manager is responsible for decisions and must make them on his own from time to time, he tries as much as possible to ensure that decision-making is a shared activity of himself and all the members of his team.

(l) Objectives for the future are agreed by group discussion wherever possible. Any orders given by the manager have at least been preceded by discussion.

(m) Quality and quantity control of work is not kept solely within the hands of the manager but is delegated so that people are to a great extent self-regulatory.

(n) Performance results are used for self-guidance by the employees and are never, ever, used in a punitive manner.

Whilst it is desirable for the manager to have an awareness of the problems of his subordinates, he does not need to be able to do all the jobs that they can do. It would not be feasible for (say) the managing director of ICI to be able to do the jobs of every single one of his employees!

One of the most significant results of the constructive style of management just outlined — and a great plus in its favour — is that it has a strong tendency to avert the formation of informal groups bent on opposing management. Such groups tend to form — perhaps a reflection of the bloody-mindedness of people — but under the ideal circumstances, the dichotomy of informal and formal group is avoided.

Action check list

☐ Study your 'leadership style'. How do others see you?

☐ List the attributes that you would like to see in your own boss (e.g. willingness to discuss problems in a constructive atmosphere) and make a sustained effort to exhibit them yourself.

Budgets, cash flow and realism

Whatever the nature and size of a business, it is imperative that managers should create, and work to, a budget and have in front of them a regularly updated cash flow forecast. There are many books on this subject and information is readily available describing a variety of ways of going about it. The important thing is to do it and not merely think about it.

Lack of a budget seems to be a problem confined largely to small-size companies, where often the attitude is that such sophistications are entirely unnecessary — a questionable precept, since evidence from the list of bankruptcies suggests that it is those companies operating on a day-to-day basis which most frequently end up broke. Budget and cash flow forecasts are notoriously absent in the building industry and it is the small builder who traditionally does not last long. There also tends to be a similar absence of these controls on the finances of small city companies and the smaller industrial manufacturers.

Maintaining a control on the inevitably limited funds available and looking ahead to determine the likely cash position in future months seems so obviously a matter of good sense that it is amazing so many people fail to do it. No doubt the manager who condemns it nevertheless applies strict control to his own personal financial situation. He is unlikely to undertake the purchase of a larger house without carefully considering whether his income is sufficient to maintain increased mortgage repayments; and his household expenditure is probably finely tuned. Yet he seems able, in business, to remain undisturbed by thoughts that there could be no cash available to pay the staff their salaries at the end of the month, or that the bank manager may find it necessary to withdraw credit facilities.

Never temper the financial truth

Anyone who considers that budgeting and cash flow forecasting is merely another example of unnecessary business technique might consider the once mighty Rolls-Royce. Though well equipped with highly qualified accountants, this organisation one day found itself unable to meet all its financial commitments. It seems reasonable to assume that some *realistic* forecasting and budgeting would have saved it from disaster. Large-size companies usually have some sort of budgeting system (often elaborate indeed) but a serious pitfall can be lack of realism.

> *'Just start from the total we want and work back!'*
> In this real-life example, accountants were constructing the sales budget for a particular chemical sold almost entirely in the United Kingdom. It so happened that 88 per cent of the sales went to twelve major users; there was a strictly limited number of suppliers and, at the time, little in the way of imports to worry about.
>
> Since the consumption capacity of the twelve major users was well known and easily checked, it was not a difficult task to calculate the maximum level of UK sales which were possible. With some knowledge of the activities of competitors, it was relatively straightforward to calculate a sales budget which could be depended on as being unusually accurate.
>
> The budget was prepared and the cash value (based on the market price of the product) was worked out. Thus, the total anticipated revenue month by month was computed and finally the whole thing, beautifully typed, was presented to the sales director The sales director looked at the document, peered at the totals, frowned, and drew a line with his pencil straight through them!
>
> He then informed the accountants that the projected earnings level was far too low to be accepted by management and should be increased by a million or two. They protested that such a decision was quite unrealistic since doing so would be to assume the company to be virtually the only supplier in the United Kingdom, and that their competitors were hardly likely to drop out of the market to suit them.
>
> The sales director stated that he was aware of this; nevertheless, he had to get the document past the Board and the best way of doing this was to start from the total that would please them and work back, calculating the amounts of the product that should be sold to various customers.

This was ultimately done and the financial planners of the company were totally misled as to the reality of life In due course this had a damaging effect in terms of investment on the manufacturing side, and adverse implications for purchase and storage of raw materials, packaging, and so on.

Lest this should be considered an isolated and unusual case of stupidity, here is another real-life case where the manager of a unit in a service industry sought advice with regard to the budget targets that had been presented to him.

The arbitrary percentage

This unit manager's masters worked on the principle that each unit of the business had to increase its revenue and profits by a given percentage each year. They had thus insisted that whatever budget he presented to them, the total revenue should be not less than 10 per cent up on the previous year's total.

It so happened that the previous year's total was very much greater than ever experienced before due to unusual circumstances. These unusual circumstances were the provision of various services for the Uganda Asians who had flooded into the country at that particular time. Since there was no possibility of another flood of Uganda Asians or anything like it, this manager had no hope of ever achieving the budget that he was forced to prepare. Having explained the circumstances — but in vain — to his bosses, the man ultimately became so disheartened and afraid of his future in the company that he resigned.

Later that year a progress check against the budget found that the company was doing even worse than might otherwise have been expected, due at least in part to the departure of an experienced and hitherto enthusiastic manager.

Controlling 'control'

Capital expenditure is another area where managers seem to go berserk either by leaning too far in the direction of control and limits, or too far in the direction of spending money like water.

An example of damaging 'control' occurred in another service industry, where it was necessary for the company to prepare quotations.

At Sprinkles Oil Installations quotations obviously had to be submitted to the potential customer within a certain time, and they invariably involved the purchase of a certain amount of capital equipment. The company were, quite reasonably, anxious to ensure that capital expenditure was well controlled but the process for doing it was so lengthy and inefficient that

47

it was never possible to get approval within less than 3 months. Indeed, all capital requirements over £50 were at that time submitted via a long chain of managers and directors to the chairman himself. Most of the people who vetted these requests were in no position to form any real judgement as to the value of the items required or their necessity to the business.

By the time approval or otherwise had been received for the capital aspects of a quotation, it was often too late to submit the quotation to the customer. Thus, a very substantial amount of business was being lost.

Too much control over expenditure can make your business unworkable.

This had been going on for some two years and consultants had a difficult job to persuade the management to modify their checking scheme so that evaluation of the project could be carried out in a more realistic time span. Management seemed almost paranoid about spending money unnecessarily and it took considerable skill to convince them that less laborious control methods could be equally effective.

Now consider the opposite problem of too casual spending. There are three test questions which managers can put to themselves when evaluating a proposal:

- Does the expenditure contribute directly or indirectly to future profits? If so, how much?
- Is there a cheaper alternative which is equally satisfactory?
- The acid-test: If I owned the business, would I spend this money?

The answers to each of these questions will go a long way towards telling the manager whether he should spend or not.

Finally, why is it that new businesses fail so often? One reason is the lack of budgeting and cash flow forecasting *before* launching into the hard, cold, commercial world. All too often a new firm will set up in a promising market with good staff and prospects only to find itself in deep trouble 12 months later. The reason is the high overheads undertaken (posh office, lavish equipment, unnecessary secretaries, luxury stationery). A calculation, in advance, would have shown whether the maximum revenue earning capacity of the firm could match the outgoings.

The same principles can apply to the launch of a new product.

Action check list

Budgets, cash flow and realism

☐ Work to a financial plan with sensible forecasts and effective controls.

☐ Be realistic in your financial planning — and don't work to figures which are politically palatable but invalid.

☐ When budgeting avoid the habit of merely adding an arbitrary percentage to last year's figures. Some thought and calculation are necessary.

☐ Don't 'over control'. Too much centralisation and bureaucracy can make your business unworkable.

10

Computers

Computers are a potentially valuable tool of business when properly applied but there are companies where this significant investment turns out to be an expensive disaster.

In the early 1960s the chairman of a large company, Garden Equipment & Tools, found himself sitting next to the chairman of another sizeable organisation, Hot Air Suppliers, at a dinner. The two began to compare notes about their companies and GET's chairman was asked what kind of computer he had. He did not know (apart from the name of the supplier) and was told by his neighbour that his organisation had acquired a new and wonderful machine which would undoubtedly solve all their problems.

GET's chairman obtained the details of the machine and subsequently ordered his computer manager to get one. (Prestige was at stake — this was the latest in computer wizardry.) The computer manager pointed out the technical reasons why the machine in question was the wrong choice for the company but the chairman, who did not understand, refused to agree. The computer manager explained the cost and disturbance aspects of the change but the chairman was not to be moved.

In due course the equipment was delivered, installed in a new computer room (alongside the room housing the old machine) and left under a plastic sheet. Two years later it was removed by a very embarrassed supplier, having never been used.

Naturally, this real-life example has been simplified (and the company names disguised!) but it illustrates an oft repeated fault — acquiring a computer without proper study.

Your company's valuable tool or its 'white elephant'?

Here are some simple observations relating to computers and their use which, if properly considered, will enable you to avoid the most common problems.

1. *Obtaining a computer*
   (a) Order your computer (this keeps the enthusiasts and the suppliers happy) and start tidying up your manual systems in readiness. Having completed the tidying up process (using a good Organisation and Methods person), you may have achieved the improvements you wanted. The order can then be cancelled and a lot of money saved.
   (b) If you are not so lucky and you still have problems (or a persistent chairman), do consider effects on
       — costs
       — staff (you may well end up with more!)
       — organisation

       Above all employ the services of a real expert to plan your systems and general set-up. Do *not* leave it to the supplier; remember his salesman is probably on commission.

2. *Controlling the computer function*
   (a) Make sure that *all* (yes, *all*) managers learn what a computer is, how it works, its limitations. When it comes to computers, managers tend to fall into two categories: those who think they know and those who don't want to know. The former make absurd and damaging demands and the latter abdicate their responsibilities to a young computer systems analyst (or an even younger programmer). Your computer systems can dominate your business policy if you don't watch out.
   (b) Do not put the computer under the control of the Chief Accountant. Accountants are not all computer experts and the chances are that the CA will use the computer exclusively for bookkeeping. Place the computer under the charge of a computer professional, reporting direct to Board level.
   (c) Decide what you want to do with the computer — objectives again — and employ the machine on profit-making applications. Find those things that ideally you need to do which are too complex

or take too long for a member of staff. In other words give support to your production planners rather than your trainee ledger clerk.

(d) Do not allow directors to get involved (unless it is the director appointed to do so).

Computer systems can dominate if you don't watch out!

3. *Finding your expert*

Failed accounts clerks, aged clerical supervisors and tired sales representatives rarely make good systems designers — and certainly not after a two-day seminar at a supplier's training school.

Computing requires a lot of know-how and a real professional will have a technical knowledge based on some years of experience *plus* a good knowledge of business. If you have no one in the company who is good enough then look outside.

Micro- and mini-computers

Don't imagine that simply because micro- and mini-computers are small the potential problems are any smaller. In some respects the problems can be greater when using this type of equipment. Expert advice (independent of the supplier) is essential and control is vital.

Some small machines can be applied in a 'dedicated' fashion to do one job — production scheduling for instance. Similarly there are machines designed to provide a range of services, such as accounting, for the small business. The danger lies in confusing the situation and ending up with an expensive toy for the production scheduler which, perhaps to obtain cost justification, is then applied willy-nilly to all sorts of unsuitable jobs. Similarly a machine may be purchased along with a whole package of applications, when only one or two are really worthwhile.

A word on word processors

Word processors are not computers despite being part of the electronic 'family' of machines. However, many of the caveats applying to computers also apply to word processors and some do's and don't's are worth mentioning.

DO — Find out the applications and the extent of them *before* buying and installing a machine.

— Appoint and train an operator and employ him or her solely as an operator.

— Have a standby operator.

— Make word processing a central service with controls on work input.

DON'T — Expect your word processor to carry out tasks which a computer should do.

— Give a machine to everyone who asks for one — apart from the benefits of a central service each machine must be cost justified. This means achieving savings or other benefits equal, each year, to purchase, servicing and maintenance costs.

Action check list

☐ Learn something about computers before using them.

☐ Don't implement computer systems merely to keep up with the Joneses.

☐ Plan and control your computer function.

☐ Ensure that your computer department is staffed by professionals and is independent of any particular division or department.

11

Concentrating on what matters

All managers are prone to allow urgent day-to-day matters to take priority over more important issues. Very often this is a result of the extreme pressures of business life, and is one reason why forward planning takes a back seat.

There is a well-known story of the Board of Directors that assembled and spent the first five minutes on reaching agreement to build a new factory costing millions of pounds; they then spent the rest of the day arguing as to whether or not ping-pong balls should be provided for the social club at the company expense.

This particular story may be apocryphal but any experienced executive will be able to recall similar examples, for it is certainly true that people prefer to talk about the things they can most easily understand. An actual example comes from *The Daily Telegraph* (2 October 1980):

> 'My spy on Sark reports that at the Michaelmas meeting of the chief Pleas, the smallest parliament in the Commonwealth, the 31 members voted unanimously and in a matter of seconds for the entry of Greece into the Common Market. The next item on the agenda, however, was the employment of a new school cleaner, which, with other weighty problems such as the desirability of a Sunday boat service, took the session well past lunchtime.'

In business, managers must concentrate on managing and not spend a disproportionate amount of their time on matters which will have very little impact on the business. This problem extends to the tendency of some managers — particularly those who have not been trained to be managers — to continue to do their previous work rather than delegating it to their subordinates. A tragic example was the case of Randolph Scrip:

Scrip was an expert insurance technician, highly proficient at dealing with problems of policy wording and skilled at matters relating to clauses, rules and regulations. His ability and hard work earned him promotion, and Randolph Scrip was placed in charge of a department of about 80 people including a number of subordinate supervisors of the various sections.

Scrip spent most of his time in his own office, alone, dealing with difficult technical matters which he felt could not be dealt with by any of his subordinates. He made no attempt to train them to do this work. Instead, Scrip took refuge in it. The work continued to give him much personal satisfaction and he felt quite content, even secure, in carrying it out; but he neglected the running of his department.

Soon, his staff became disorganised and demoralised: They did not recognise Scrip as their leader, and they had no objectives. There were no controls over the quality or quantity of work that passed through the department, no standards of performance were laid down, proper communication between top management and the clerical levels fizzled out, and absolutely no thought was given to forward planning.

Scrip became involved in the matters of management only when a situation had reached crisis point and he had no alternative. This became most noticeable whenever one of his staff resigned or retired as, having made no forward plans to cater for such events, Scrip would have to take emergency action to deal with the vacancy — not to mention the consequent overload of work on other staff.

Action check list

☐ Decide what are the most important matters in your job: they must be those that will make a big impact on the business.

☐ Make sure you are concentrating on those matters rather than spending too much time on the easier, often trivial, day-to-day issues.

☐ Remember that if you are a manager you should be *managing* and delegating as much work as possible to your subordinates while maintaining control over the quality and quantity of work they do.

☐ Train your staff to cope with difficult technical matters and try to avoid doing your previous work yourself.

12

Avoiding decisions

For a variety of reasons — not necessarily because the issue is complex — some managers find it difficult to take decisions. They appear to be unwilling to commit themselves to a particular line of action, perhaps because by doing so reputations may be placed in jeopardy and a decision means moving in a new direction or accepting a new philosophy.

This unwillingness to take decisions can lead to a fascinating range of avoidance actions, of which the classic one is to pass the problem to a colleague or an unfortunate subordinate to deal with. Such action is fairly obvious to the victim and bystanders, and indecisive managers adopt numerous ingenious tactics to avoid the issues. Some of the methods are so subtle that even the manager himself may not be aware that he is taking refuge behind avoidance action. Unconsciously, the manager's motive is to avoid taking responsibility.

A selection of avoidance actions

Readers may well be familiar with some of these frequent forms of evasion!

1. *The top man's favourite*
Appoint a committee to study the issue. This gives the impression of acting in a very responsible manner, showing that the big boss is not going to take an ill-considered action or act impetuously.

In practice, the selection of the committee will take some time and it may be weeks before the appointed members find a convenient moment to convene their first meeting. With luck the subject will be totally dead before the committee actually meets. If not, any recommendation it makes to the big boss can be safely accepted by him. Should the recommendation prove to be an error, he can always blame it on the committee.

2. *The future agenda technique*

An item is raised (usually as 'any other business') at a routine meeting and there is an inclination on the part of those present to defer discussion which means, of course, deferring a decision. Usually someone suggests that more time is needed to consider the matter fully and that the item should be put on the agenda for a future meeting. Skilful manipulations of the minutes and/or the agenda for the next meeting can sometimes contrive to ensure that the subject disappears entirely, and at least the whole thing has been delayed for a few weeks!

3. *Send for the Marines*

Make a fervent and elaborate case for consulting an expert on virtually any subject that might crop up. This approach (which is, incidentally, costly) has considerable attraction as a form of delaying action and shifting the burden of responsibility elsewhere. The expert first has to be identified and found (probably from outside the company) and some time will elapse before he is available to look at the problem. Having looked at it briefly, he will then indicate his likely fee for the work to be done. At this stage it is possible for someone to query the size of the fee and suggest that it is exorbitant. Thus, by gentle stages, the whole subject can be pushed into oblivion.

4. *The too busy ploy*

A characteristic of this particular move is that someone expresses anxiety that the matter be firmly and positively dealt with; the necessity to make a decision is heavily underlined but the point is made that it would be more prudent to deal with the issue when everyone is less busy.

This is a time which will never actually come round since we are all busy and there is no shortage of 'inappropriate' times during the year. For example, we shall be less busy when the auditors have completed their work/the financial year end has been concluded/the quarterly and half year end work finished/the holiday season is over/Christmas and New Year are behind us. The seasonal rush of business is also a stumbling block and (scratching the bottom of the barrel) there are such things as the annual dinner dance, the Chairman's annual golf match, and the sales department conference to get through first. The busy period leading up to the Annual General Meeting should also be avoided and in any case we may have to wait till Tomkinson returns from his Far East trip!

5. *The Rip Van Winkle gambit*
This seems to be a favourite of the man who smokes a pipe. The meeting is held up for a minute or two waiting for the pipe-smoker's reply, during which time the pipe is laboriously packed with tobacco and sundry matches are consumed in lighting it. Having then given an impression of serious contemplation during the pipe-filling period, the pipe-smoker intones with an air of wisdom that this is one of those questions which should be slept on. The sleeping period can be somewhat lengthy and time will be needed to set up a new meeting which, if carefully planned, can be found to clash with the year end/the auditors/the golf match . . . see the 'Too busy ploy'!

By means such as these, people can duck out of an enormous range of issues, often for long enough for it to be too late to make a decision anyway.

Decisions commonly ducked

The following is a selection of carefully avoided decisions, all taken from real life, and revealing the wide variety of problems which managements choose to ignore.

1. The relocation of the company
   The idea had enormous potential savings for the company and considerable benefits for the staff. It was generally believed that the very senior man who successfully blocked a final decision on this question was in fact acting on the instructions of his wife who was not at all keen to move to a new place.
2. A new salaries and wages scheme
   This was extremely important to the staff, not merely because some felt that they were sadly underpaid, but to ensure that anomalies in the wage

structure were removed. The issue had implications for the future prosperity of the firm as well.

3. A technical training scheme

   This was seriously overdue as quality of work was being adversely affected by a lack of know-how in certain key areas. Probably the motivation behind the avoidance action was lack of confidence on the part of the person likely to have charge of the training scheme. He doubted that he could cope with it.

4. A computer application.

5. Dealing with a staff complaint

   Staff complaints should always be dealt with promptly and effectively. Leaving any grievance, whether real or imagined, unanswered can guarantee that the wound will fester and become contagious.

6. Implementing agreed organisational changes

   Although the organisational changes were officially accepted as being desirable, blocking action was observed from those who felt that they would be worse off as a result.

7. Allocation of car parking spaces

   This is always a hairy problem in cases where there are not enough spaces to go round (see p. 90 'The status symbol syndrome').

8. Reviewing sales prices.

9. Accepting or rejecting a marginally profitable order

   In this particular case personal pride was at stake since a senior person on the sales side had negotiated a potential order which was border-line from a profit point of view. He was anxious that the order should be accepted to safeguard his reputation, whilst some of his rivals were keen to demonstrate that his negotiation had been rather poorly conducted. The interests of the firm, which would have been revealed by calculations involving manufacturing costs and plant utilisation, were entirely subordinated to a battle between the interested parties and ultimately the whole thing just died out.

A ferocious but very efficient general sales manager once gave a salutary lesson to one of his young executives. The young executive had received a phone call from a customer who was considerably upset by the actions of the company and wanted to know what it was going to do about it. Unable to make his mind up as to the right response, the executive promised to ring back, but his immediate superiors were not present in the office to advise him and he shelved the problem. On the following day, he asked the advice of the general sales manager who was more than a little concerned that the matter had been ignored for 24 hours. He pointed out that the customer could reasonably expect a prompt response and asked the young executive why he had not made a decision himself. After receiving the young man's cxcuses the sales manager looked him squarely in the eyes and said: 'If you make a decision which I consider to be the wrong one I will possibly tick you off but certainly explain to you why in my view you were wrong. If, however, you fail to make a decision at all, you can be sure of one thing — I will sack you.'

Action check list

☐ Recognise that decision-making requires effort. Courage, discipline and trust may also be needed.

☐ Avoid the temptations of spurious 'excuses' such as setting up study groups, committees etc. Delay is only justified by a genuine lack of factual information.

13

Organisation

In the London office of an international company where a total of 198 people were employed, seven of the executive staff had no clearly defined role. The 'magnificent seven' accounted for 3.5 per cent of the payroll costs. Six of these executives spent their time inventing work and pretending to be busy because they were aware of their lack of any real responsibilities. The seventh busily occupied himself by interfering with practically every other activity in the building, causing dissention and confusion.

Two other senior executives with similar jobs each reported to a different boss, resulting in conflicting instructions and wasted time, hampered by delays arising from the psychological need of the weaker of the two bosses to make his influence felt on every possible occasion. (In fact, his involvement was rarely required but, not unnaturally, he was unwilling to admit it.)

One administrative function was split into two parts reporting to different managers, and a third senior executive on the commercial side of the business was responsible for one minor part of the same administration scene.

Thus perhaps 10 per cent of the executive staff worked in roles that were not defined, or were so badly defined that confusion and quarrels were inevitable. There may well have been similar anomalies relating to the clerical, secretarial and other non-executive staff to aggravate the general situation. Here is a classic case of deplorable business organisation: lack of clear responsibilities, fuzzy demarcations of authority, and job descriptions with no meaning.

Defining the organisational structure

If managements wish to avoid wasting the skills at their disposal then a clear organisational structure is essential.

Starting at the top, managements must decide whether they will go for a functional type of operation or a divisional type. There are many sources of information on this subject but it is worth mentioning here that the functional split has separate and distinct departments — for production, sales, etc. — all under directors who normally report to the managing director; while the divisional system is one involving the profit centre concept, in which various elements of the business in respect to a particular product — for example, production, sales, accounting, research — are grouped all under one executive.

The functional system tends to give rise to a considerable number of disadvantages including the following:

(a) The structure inhibits response to product diversification or other marketing opportunities since the head of each function is inevitably forced into a parochial position. There is no one apart from the managing director himself who can take an overall view in respect of any particular product.

(b) Profit responsibility rests solely on the managing director; his subordinates are far more concerned with looking after their own sectional interests — interests, incidentally, which are often in conflict. In other words, entrepreneurial and imaginative action is positively discouraged.

(c) The scope for succession and management development is limited since each executive is confined to his own field of sales, production or whatever and has little opportunity to be exposed to other fields.

(d) The managing director (who, it seems, normally comes up from sales or accounting) tends to favour the function from which he came. This is understandable as it is likely to be the function that he understands best and he will arrive in the managing director's chair with a conviction that that function is the most important in the company.

The divisional structure on the other hand does allow responsibility for profit to be delegated, allows a separate evaluation of the firm's main activities and generally is more motivating for middle management.

There is also more scope for management development and major decisions are taken near the point of action, leaving the managing director time for planning ahead which should be his number one function in life.

Thus the divisional set-up tends to encourage entrepreneurial action and is altogether a more exciting framework within which to work.

Some pitfalls in weak organisation

There are a number of hybrid versions of organisational framework which can suit various types of business, but the most important thing of all is that there should be *some* form of defined organisational structure — almost any kind is better than none at all! Managements who fail to define their structure or allocate responsibilities clearly will find that the more energetic and dominant personalities will form an informal structure of command which may well work against the interests of the business rather than for it. Most people finding themselves in a vacuum tend to work towards their own personal and narrow interests.

Lack of clear job descriptions not only creates a miserable state of affairs for the individual, who wonders what he is really supposed to be doing, but it also encourages top management to dabble in lower-level activities when they should be getting on with the strategic and other high-level requirements of the organisation.

A long-encouraged myth is the notion of the 'span of command'. For many years textbooks informed us that each manager should ideally have five people reporting to him (that is, five lower-level managers). Some organisations have blindly adhered to this principle which, when rigidly applied, can cause all kinds of problems.

It does not really matter how many people report to an individual boss provided that he can be available to help in any of his areas to the degree necessary. Thus a manager may have reporting to him only two subordinates, each running a very active department, requiring a great deal of support. Another manager may have as many as ten functions reporting to him of which perhaps six or seven virtually run themselves and require very little active supervision.

Other dangers which can emerge from absence of structure include lack of succession planning: that is, no up and coming youngsters providing management in depth. Territorial jealousies develop between the conflicting interests and this encourages some departmental managers to be in a permanent state of war with one or more of their colleagues.

The promotional ladder

One of the great difficulties of organisational structure is that of providing the so-called promotional ladder. Some managements are rightly concerned to ensure that their younger staff can see a way to the top to satisfy their ambitions. Structures are therefore defined to reveal a ladder of positions ascending to the chairman's office. This is laudable, but management must grasp one fact: ladder or no ladder, promotion which depends entirely on 'dead man's shoes' is not at all encouraging to the young executive. Real and rapid promotion can arise only from expansion of the business to create more management functions. This in turn must be linked to a positive and continuous plan of individual development and manpower planning in order to ensure that future executive requirements are adequately identified, and that individuals can see that they have a reasonable chance of progress.

Beware the 'honours list'!

It is a common practice in the City of London to award spurious titles to long-serving individuals dressed up as a form of promotion. Thus one can find in broker's offices and insurance companies aged clerical staff with grandiose titles such as assistant director, executive director, associate director. To the initiated these titles have no meaning whatsoever. The titles are conferred but the employees so honoured are quickly made to realise that they should continue with their functions as before, and are not required to contribute to the management or direction of the business.

This form of promotion may please staff at the receiving end initially but disillusionment soon follows and a truly ambitious and energetic executive hampered by an empty title becomes even more disenchanted with his lot. Only the more turgid employee — invariably a mediocre type — kids himself that he has really made it and can remain motivated by such an award. Thus it proves to be merely another means of encouraging mediocrity since those in the latter category stay with the organisation and those who are energetic and ambitious will move on. Like job descriptions, therefore, titles must be meaningful not only for the sake of the individuals concerned but for the effectiveness of the business.

Action check list

- [ ] A good organisation will provide a 'framework' for the business — which otherwise will be prone to chaos and wasted effort.

- [ ] Decide on the organisational structure which suits your company — for instance, a structure that encourages, rather than inhibits, decision-making.

- [ ] Remember that almost any recognisable structure is better than none but do avoid meaningless titles and status symbol functions.

14

Communicating

In every business organisation there are employees who at some time will state that the company they work for is bad at communicating.

Give it to them straight!

Management benefits from using straightforward communication techniques. A number of observations can be made:

1. *Avoid pseudo-secrecy*
Tell people as much as they can possibly be told regarding the events inside and outside the company which affect both the company and its employees. Pseudo-secrecy should be avoided. There is a tendency for managers, having made a decision, to say to each other 'This is a confidential matter which must not be made known outside these four walls'. Yet, invariably, an objective analysis of this statement reveals it to be absolute nonsense and merely a way of boosting the importance of the people present.

2. *Establish a procedure for communication*
Utilising regular departmental meetings and notice boards is vital. Management should report directly to their staff and not via shop stewards. When reporting is done by shop stewards, the message could be distorted to become the one which the shop steward himself thinks

should be passed on. In any event, it will be given his personal slant and tone of voice and if the procedure is repeated regularly the employees will begin to regard the shop steward as the boss, and pay less regard to the management of the company.

3. *Make the message understandable*

This may seem obvious but just consider the following quotation from a notice, given to employees in a well-known British company, and designed to explain the awards to individuals under the profit-earning bonus scheme. The first paragraph of the announcement explained the value of each person's share units in the scheme and then went on:

'The year's results are rather disappointing. They reflect the limited effects of reflationary actions in the world in general and the UK in particular,

Is your message understandable?

where it has proved difficult to secure real growth without putting excessive pressure on the rate of inflation or on the balance of payments.'

This statement was directed at every employee ranging from those with a good knowledge of finance and international economics to the great majority with very little understanding of such matters.

In this instance, a survey of 50 employees was conducted to ascertain their understanding of that particular paragraph; not one of them had understood it. They were, however, extremely interested in the amount of bonus due to them, and most made some comment to the effect that whilst they couldn't understand the paragraph concerned, they weren't the slightest bit interested in it either! In other words, the manager who wrote it had failed to convey anything of relevance to the staff. Ironically, this occurred in an organisation which prided itself on the care that it took over its communications to employees. This example of showing off by using big words is a trap that many managers fall into, particularly managers who have not been taught how to communicate.

The rumour network

One thing is certain: if no communication is made on some official basis, then a communication will go round on an unofficial basis. The rumour network in any organisation is strong and invariably damaging.

When a story goes round, the optimists assume that they will benefit from whatever is being talked about and the pessimists assume that they will suffer from it. The former become disenchanted when they find that they are not benefiting from increased salaries, bonuses, company cars or whatever; and the pessimists are confirmed in their original misery. Thus nothing positive ensues.

A senior manager, leading a large department, once complained of the existence of a management committee of which he was not a member. The committee met each week and, although they kept minutes of each meeting, these were never published.

The manager concerned was disturbed by the secrecy and possibly felt threatened by it. He commented 'Goodness knows what they are talking about and what decisions they are taking'. He imagined all kinds of sinister goings-on — and assumed that whatever was decided had to be bad for him.

Some weeks later the committee was persuaded to invite the worried manager to join them as he had much valuable expertise to offer. In due course, he commented, 'Those meetings are boring! Nothing of real significance is ever discussed!'

Action check list

☐ Inform your staff as much as you possibly can, as soon as you can, on every aspect of the business.

☐ Create a 'system' for communication to ensure that it *is* done and as effectively as possible.

15

System

A primary requirement for a manager is to have a system to cover the work that his department is responsible for; this will ensure that there are laid-down procedures which, even if not perfect, at least serve as guidelines. Too often there are no agreed formal procedures at all. This allows individuals to do exactly as they like, which inevitably ends up in waste of time and unnecessary work.

Lack of system creates a vacuum which can be easily filled with anarchy.

Will it work?

Having agreed a system it is important that this is regularly reviewed with the people who operate it to ensure that it remains up to date and fits the changing work scene. Innumerable cases are reported in business journals and at O & M seminars of systems so old that they are now entirely inapplicable to the present day situation yet still adhered to by managers with a tenacity that is mind-boggling! Frequently forms designed some years before (when circumstances were different) are still in use and causing extra work. Naturally if a clerk is given a form to fill in, and the form includes unnecessary columns or entries, there is a good chance that the unnecessary data will be carefully dug out and inserted on the form — extra work not only for the clerk but also for the next person reading the form and trying to make some sense of it. It is far from uncommon to find Department X filling in forms and sending them to Department Y with all kinds of information that is not actually required. Oddly enough, the latter department rarely mentions it to the former.

The converse can also apply: the receiving department may feel utterly frustrated when they do not receive information they need on a routine basis, simply because there is no space on the form for the sender to insert it.

It is a manager's responsibility to review these situations from time to time and to ensure that systems are brought up to date at least once a year.

Is it correctly operated?

Another common mistake is to confuse lack of discipline with lack of an adequate system. Departmental managers have been known to criticise a system for not working properly or for being grossly inadequate. Yet nothing is found to be wrong with the system: the real problem proves to be that staff (including the managers themselves) consistently fail to follow the system as laid down. No system will work properly unless the people who operate it do so faithfully and correctly. As soon as one person steps out of line and breaks the procedure, others have to do likewise in order to keep the process going. In time, the variations built in by individuals become part of a new (informal) system which soon becomes unwieldy, difficult to understand and the cause of disputes and disagreements.

This kind of situation is particularly common amongst sales staff, many of whom tend to regard any kind of discipline as a waste of their time and rather beneath their dignity. But it is by no means confined to sales staff. Every manager should ask himself whether or not this situation exists in his own area of operations.

At Grabbitts, where this lack of discipline was pin-pointed, the managers agreed to enforce adherence to the system. However, they failed to carry it through and a few weeks later were still insisting that the system was no good and should be replaced. They were duly provided with a new system — a variation on the original one which made little practical difference — in the hope that, given a fresh start, they would continue in a proper fashion. They again failed to maintain correct procedures and again the system was abused as being inadequate. It was a hard task convincing the executives and managers of their own shortcomings, and that the situation could only be saved if, in spite of the pressures of the day, they adhered rigidly to the system.

Good managers must be aware of procedures that are starting to slip and should take steps to retrieve them before a new (informal) system becomes an ingrained habit.

At the Alphabet Company, Department A demanded an investigation into why certain data received from Department B was seldom correct, rarely complete, and irregular in arriving. It was discovered that although Department B had a perfectly adequate system there were people not adhering to it. However, during the course of the investigations the staff, becoming aware that their work was under scrutiny, began to follow the system more closely, and things began to improve of themselves — to the extent that, after a few weeks, the manager of Department A commented on the wonderful new system introduced into Department B which had resulted in a much better flow of work to his department! Fortunately, when the state of play was fully explained to the two managers concerned they immediately took the point, and imposed tighter discipline with a satisfactory long-term result.

Sometimes a perfectly good system can be made unworkable by one small weakness in it — this weakness often caused by lack of care on the part of the manager, as in this real-life example:

In Toggle and Company's factory there was an elaborate and expensive production planning system. The system was, if anything, too elaborate and too expensive but nevertheless should have worked satisfactorily — though it never did. Careful investigation showed that the cause of the trouble was, literally, the lack of a small table on the shop floor! Sundry documents had to be assembled and sorted out in this area as part of the process leading up to controlling production on the machines. The person on the shop floor responsible for this job had absolutely nowhere to keep these papers, nowhere to sort them and sift them; dozens of carefully prepared forms were simply heaped together in a greasy mess on a work bench which otherwise housed bits of metal, spare parts and tools.

When this man was provided with a suitable table and one or two filing trays in a corner of the workshop, the whole problem disappeared.

This is perhaps an extreme example but it does illustrate very well a situation that is only too commonly found.

Action check list

☐ Effective ways of working are unlikely to evolve by accident. Carefully thought out systems are essential.

☐ Review your systems regularly.

☐ Ensure that systems are adhered to and that staff understand why this is necessary.

16

Salaries and other rewards

Almost everyone in business and elsewhere would agree that reward should be linked to achievement, as this is not only a motivating factor but also a way of providing just recognition of an individual's services.

Whilst a great deal of lip service is paid to this principle, there are too many cases where in reality it does not apply. All too often, salary awards are made by an anonymous body of people — sometimes by one person only — equipped with few, if any, of the relevant facts that would enable them to determine the value of an individual and reward accordingly.

Fair and 'seen to be fair'

An example of this involved a committee of two men who each year decided the salary increases to be awarded to a staff of about 400. Their method was to work their way through the list of names, one by one, awarding to the unknown majority a standard 'across the board' increase; whenever they came to a familiar name, however, they tended to decide on a different figure. Thus any individual who had drawn favourable attention to himself in the weeks preceding this exercise was almost sure to receive a higher increase in salary than the majority.

The two-man committee knew that this was a hit-or-miss process and accepted a recommendation that salary awards should be, at least in part, based on reports from departmental managers. Unfortunately, no organised system was laid down at the outset and, as a consequence, when salaries were next reviewed it was on the basis of a collection of inconsistently worded notes from some managers and no information at all from others. No attempt was made to ensure that each manager sent in a sensible report on each of his members of staff with an appropriate recommendation. Nor was any standard form used so that the various attributes of each person could be considered and each given equal treatment. Apparently the departmental managers had been wholly opposed to this approach on the basis that it represented more paperwork. Since the reports were left to individual managers as a free choice, some took care and tried to produce just and fair reports, while others merely jotted down the first few comments that they could think of.

A simple form to complete would, at least, have provided a check list of points to consider such as: time-keeping, quality of work, enthusiasm, and willingness to cooperate with colleagues.

Staff need to know that they are being dealt with on a fair and 'seen to be fair' basis otherwise, inevitably, many will regard themselves as unfairly paid compared with others. In other words, a standard procedure must be laid down and made known to every person in the organisation. The procedure must then be followed with considerable discipline to ensure as fair a result as possible.

Some companies, quite rightly, take the trouble to work out scales of salary and have a carefully worked out mathematical approach to salaries, linked to job evaluation schemes and the like. Not all organisations will find this more sophisticated approach suitable for them, but they should at least apply something fairer than the 'by guess or by God' approach.

Don't under-value the 'back-room' boys

An area which can lead to substantial staff dissatisfaction is the bonus scheme. Many companies pay their employees an annual bonus — often a relic of the Victorian idea of dishing out a chicken and a bottle of sherry at Christmas time.

Perhaps the simplest and fairest approach is to give each individual a bonus based on a percentage of salary, this percentage being the same for everyone and based on the published results of the company's year of trading. By this means, everyone knows that the bonus is linked to overall results, and that each person is treated equally.

It may be desirable in some cases to select certain individuals who have contributed an unusually great amount to the company during the year, and to give them an additional ex gratia payment on top of the standard bonus. Many companies do this but tend to spoil it by always choosing front line staff for the most generous awards. Thus, some bright, smooth-tongued young salesperson who landed one good sale shortly before the bonus awards were worked out is liable to come off extremely well. By contrast the conscientious post room supervisor, say, beavering away throughout the year and saving the company much aggravation from minor problems gets nothing. Diligence is not glamorous and he is unlikely to draw attention to himself.

> This situation existed at Scrunchers, a broking company. Each year the brokers who went into the market received enormous bonuses compared with their less fortunate colleagues who manned the office. An examination of the quality of the work carried out by some of these brokers, however, revealed that they were often slapdash and lazy. Their paperwork was wholly inadequate to provide a good customer service and it was left to the clerks in the office to straighten things out, get the right facts and to ensure that ultimately the customer was satisfied. However, there was no glamour in the office clerks' job and the senior management (all brokers themselves) regarded their function with little interest. Marked changes in attitude started to emerge only when, as part of a new training scheme, some of the brokers began to work in the office and could thus appreciate the important contribution made by the office staff to the success of the company.

This type of approach is to be recommended in many situations.

Misapplying appraisal schemes

Another serious failure in salary awards is to link salary with company appraisal schemes. Appraisal schemes are intended solely for the purpose of looking ahead in terms of an individual's career — to provide a means of identifying strengths and weaknesses so that this awareness may be utilised to develop a more effective staff, capable of better things — and as closely in line as possible with the personal ambitions of each individual.

If the annual appraisal interview is known to be linked with the annual salary award then it is inevitable that the individual being appraised will be reluctant to admit to any weaknesses or failings on his own part. Appraisal schemes misused in this way are likely to fall by the wayside, thus wasting an opportunity for a company to develop its human assets to the best advantage and to give its people a chance of a more productive, prosperous and satisfactory career.

Action check list

☐ Salaries should reflect an employee's value and not be the result of arbitrary decisions.

☐ A *procedure* for salary review and awards is essential.

☐ The salary procedures must be fair and seen to be so. Avoid giving the lion's share to the people in glamorous jobs.

☐ Do not link salary awards to appraisal schemes.

17

Manager traps

There are a number of regular and routine traps that a manager can fall into and the following are some of the most common and the most disastrous.

The 'I know best' syndrome

The person who is unwilling to delegate is often the same person who insists on checking everything. In other words, whatever work his staff do he insists on checking it himself before regarding it as completed. This final check is even applied to writing letters, where the use of certain terms or grammatical constructions can be a question of personal taste and it is unlikely that two individuals would have exactly the same approach.

> The sales office of the Treeleaf Company comprised half a dozen executives, but the boss insisted on reading every letter written to their many customers before despatch. Not surprisingly, productivity was low since the manager invariably found something to criticise (perhaps the absence of a comma!) and almost every letter required minor alterations. As a result, the secretaries were grossly overworked and the executives more and more demoralised. It was a situation where half the number of staff could have coped with the work if the manager had been able to trust their judgement and to accept that slight mistakes occasionally occur in every organisation.

It is this type of manager who decides that he cannot take his holidays lest the company come to a disastrous standstill during his absence.

But it really means that either he is so conceited that he cannot imagine how the firm can keep going without him; or he has completely failed to train his staff to run the department in his absence; or he cannot trust his colleagues to look after the business while he is away. His staff, on the other hand, may long for the boss to disappear on holiday so that they have a chance to get on with their work in peace — not a chance to slacken off or waste time.

The 'I must approve' syndrome

Although managers must keep a sensitive finger on the pulse, they should do this judiciously and discreetly, and must be careful to avoid self-defeating actions which create an atmosphere of derision.

> The managing director of Jam Pot Covers Inc., in an effort to curb unnecessary expenditure, issued an instruction that all future expenditure must be approved by himself. His instruction placed no lower limit on this, and when it was queried whether or not he wished to approve all items of expenditure, however trivial, he confirmed that this was indeed his intention. It was subsequently calculated that to obtain approval for the purchase of an item costing around £1.00 involved at least six times that much expenditure in executive time.

Carrying controls to such lengths merely brings the whole concept into disrepute and causes frustration all down the line — reactions which may eventually develop into constant sneering at top management and an unhealthy cynicism.

The 'I must know' syndrome

Certain managers seem unable to carry out their functions, or indeed survive from day to day, without acquiring every imaginable bit of information produced by the company.

Now that computers are in widespread use it is tempting for a manager to insist on a copy of each and every print-out, however technical its data or obscure its application. But does the manager really need this information, or is it merely the fact of being on the list of recipients that makes him feel secure and important? The cost of producing information can be substantial; the cost of reading it and storing it can also be significant.

> The new manager of Brimful's computer department, going through all the various listings and reports which were produced and despatched to various people, came across one substantial report of around 300 pages, the purpose of which was baffling. Upon investigation he discovered that these reports were sent to an entirely different company down the road who proceeded to bind them in a special binder and then return them to his department. No one could explain why this was done, or why the other company was involved, or indeed what the purpose of this exercise was. The supervisor of the binding operation was also unable to explain it. He knew only that this had been going on for three or four years, that they received no fee for the binding job, that the information was of absolutely no interest to his company, and that he would be delighted to see this onerous task removed from his office!
>
> Of the four copies produced and carefully bound, three were stored without anyone actually reading them and the fourth was sent to the Chairman of the company. The new manager therefore went to the Chairman's office to ask whether the report was essential information. There he encountered the Secretary Barrier (see p. 88) and was firmly informed that it was vital that the Chairman received his reports regularly each month, and that the information therein was important. However, in the course of this conversation, the alert manager noticed, on the top of some cupboards, previous issues of the report in question looking conspicuously untouched, and he became suspicious that the Chairman had never actually opened any of these. He therefore instructed the computer department to produce the documents for the next three months in the usual way but not to send them for binding, nor to the Chairman. Since, at the end of the three months, neither the Chairman nor his secretary had given any indication that this information had been missed, he concluded that the Chairman did not use it. Subsequently the manager found an opportunity to ask the Chairman about the report; the latter denied all knowledge of it, saying that he couldn't imagine what possible purpose it could serve.

Any manager who is in doubt as to whether or not he needs some particular piece of information should ask the acid-test question: Does any action result from the production of this information or from my receipt of it? If the answer is no, then he should suppress the report in question.

The secretary barrier

Those managers who tell their staff that their door is always open are not infrequently the same managers who place a secretary between themselves and their staff, to intercept all phone calls and visitors and decide who and what should be presented to the boss. The manager has thus delegated to his secretary the power to decide which subjects require priority. Obviously the more senior the man the more dangerous is this form of delegation.

One of the most ludicrous aspects of British business is the simple telephone call from one company to another. The sequence of events involves Mr Cox asking his secretary to put through a call to Mr Box at the other company. His secretary dials the number and asks the telephonist for Mr Box. She is then put through to Mr Box's secretary and the two of them hold a brief discussion prior to Box's secretary enquiring of him whether he can take a call from Mr Cox. Mr Box agrees and his secretary then speaks to Cox's secretary who in turn relays the information to Mr Cox. Eventually, the two men are ready to converse. But how much simpler and cheaper it would have been for Mr Cox to ring Mr Box direct.

Promoting the wrong person

There is considerable temptation, when a vacancy occurs, to promote the longest-serving employee in the group. This long-serving employee is usually well-informed technically, and so he is made the new supervisor, manager or whatever.

The fact is that to be a good manager, technical knowledge and years of service are not enough. The person selected must have the personality and capability to lead others, to organise work, and to communicate in order to succeed. Many good departments have gone downhill and, alas, numerous hitherto happy and successful employees have been made thoroughly miserable, because of unwise promotion.

Then there are those who err in the opposite direction and make the mistake of assuming that none of the existing staff will ever be good enough to fill the promotion vacancy. They therefore look — at considerable expense — outside the company. Certainly this is sometimes necessary and justified; but it is a quirk of human nature that often people we know well appear to lack potential, whereas the applicant from outside may be regarded as the answer to a manager's prayer. It is salutary to bear in mind that the person from outside may also have been regarded by his former colleagues as run-of-the-mill; the chances are that they were astonished when he joined your company in a new and more senior role!

Waiting for the decision

Decisions are not always taken as and when we desire or require them. This can be particularly frustrating when from a manager's point of view the decision to be taken seems obvious. Many a manager grows to accept lengthy periods of frustration; after all, even if he can see the damage being done he can safely blame it on the lack of a decision from above. But this is weak; some action is called for, to avoid such a situation.

It is usually best to get on and do the job required. If necessary, a memo may be prepared in advance and sent to the decision-makers, informing them: 'If by such and such a time I have not received instructions to the contrary, I propose to do the following.' This action is unlikely to create any problems — rather the reverse — since the majority of delayed decisions are those which people either do not understand or do not wish to get involved in; thus the decision-makers are more than delighted when an individual takes the responsibility on his own shoulders and saves them the trouble!

The absent VIP

Many companies have an executive floor in their office buildings in which sit the great captains of the industry concerned. It may be tempting to shut ourselves away from the hard, cruel world and to enjoy the comforts of the executive suite; but this is not good management.

One Christmas time, the managing director of Popcorn International decided to descend from his ivory tower and take a stroll around the offices of the other staff. He was upset when few people paid him any attention and he brought this to the notice of his administration committee. It was gently pointed out to him that he had never before walked round the office, that his only contacts were with the senior heads of department, and that he even had his own private entrance into the building to spare him coming in with the rest of the staff; so he was paid little attention because he was not recognised.

No man should regard himself as a leader if his staff do not even know his face.

The status symbol syndrome

All human beings need a sense of status in order to feel happy, and it is human nature to try to develop it. However, the good manager will be very careful indeed how he goes about this because over emphasising status symbols can be extremely damaging and can make otherwise competent people appear as fools. The following instances of status symbols are based on real life examples.

The car space

Frequently the possession of a car space — suitably labelled with the user's name or initials — is regarded as a number one status symbol. Unless the space is fully utilised, however, it can cause immense irritation to those who waste much time trying to find somewhere to park. A company is best served if its car parking spaces are allocated according to need rather than status. Thus those dealing with emergencies or computer shift staff, for example, may need a car parking facility more than the head of a department, who often travels by train anyway.

Special stationery

A certain company in London provided its staff with white blotting paper. One of the directors decided that white blotting paper was bad for his eyes because it gave off too much glare. He therefore arranged for the stationery supplies officer to provide him with a pale yellow blotting paper exclusively for his use. After a time feeling this pale yellow colour to be a good idea, he extended it to include ordinary stationery such as letter paper and envelopes. After about 12 months the stores comprised enough standard stationery for 1,100 employees and sufficient non-standard yellow stationery for one employee.

The next step was to add his own name to the company letterhead so that his letters went out on his own personal yellow paper. The backs of envelopes were similarly annotated with his name, and one might have been forgiven for believing that he himself was the company and the others merely supporting staff.

The effect of this posturing was to increase dramatically the cost of stationery for the company. Although it does not cost much to buy one special packet of blotting paper, it costs a great deal indeed to arrange special print runs for the benefit of one individual.

This desire for personalised stationery may spread throughout an organisation until virtually everyone wants paper printed with his own name — and not infrequently in his own choice of colour as well. The waste is made more apparent whenever someone enjoying this status symbol resigns, dies or otherwise departs from the scene and substantial quantities of obsolete paper are converted into scrap pads.

The wait/enter sign

An illuminated sign can be positioned outside an office and, by means of a desk control, can be made to light up the words 'Enter' or 'Wait'. This somewhat discourteous device may give the user a sense of power but is extremely annoying to those who are stopped by it. The wait sign is a time-waster because the person outside the door has no way of knowing how long the wait may be, and could hang about for some time before giving up. Meanwhile the occupant of the office may be denying himself information of some importance.

The large office

It is almost standard procedure both in business and the civil service to relate office size to rank. This is illogical. Office space is expensive and at £X per square foot should not be used to confirm that an individual has reached a certain level of importance.

The size of office allocated to *any* individual should relate to the space required to do the job satisfactorily. Thus someone who, by the nature of the job, receives many visitors may require an office larger than average to accommodate them comfortably. Similarly someone who has repeatedly to hold meetings with his subordinates or who has unwieldy computer print-outs to examine may need a generally larger office.

It is certainly a bad sign when a very large office is allocated to a manager of a department whilst his staff are hampered by having inadequate space in which to spread their papers and carry out their normal functions.

The size of the desk

Rather like the office size, the size of desk also tends to be in proportion to the rank of the user. This too is illogical and at times borders on the absurd.

Is the junior accounts clerk, who deals with large ledgers, computer print-outs or whatever, sitting at a small desk surrounded by heaps of papers piled on the floor, because the working surface is just not big enough?

Is the chairman of the company dwarfed by a desk the size of a tennis court, on which are placed (at the most) two or three pieces of paper at a time?

It is a fact that the more august the person the less likely he is to have vast quantities of paperwork so a better way of demonstrating his importance might be to equip him with a smaller and smaller desk the more important he becomes!

If only one could persuade senior management to accept a design which reflected the nature of their work — that is to say, comfortable chairs and occasional tables more suited to talking and listening than a massive desk — then it would be possible to reverse this particular status symbol.

Private lifts

In the West End of London there was, until recently, an office building which had five lifts from the ground to the top floor. Four of these lifts were for general use and the fifth was a special high speed lift restricted to directors heading for the directors' floor. Every morning frustrated crowds of employees waited to get into the four lifts while the fifth was, for most of the time, not in use.

The building had been designed for a certain number of occupants, and five lifts had been installed in order to meet their needs. By appropriating one lift the directors had not only made themselves into an exclusive club but they had also made it impossible for their staff to move quickly enough up and down the building.

Individual tea-trays and quality cups

The tradition of morning coffee and afternoon tea in British offices gives rise to a hierarchy of luxury which, like most other perks and status symbols, causes envy and discontent and makes the upper echelons appear somewhat precious.

One company has an arrangement of vending machines for the ordinary staff, a thermos flask plus mug for the next level up, a tray with small tea service for the third level; and, when one has finally reached the top, a salver complete with lace napkin, silver-plated teapot and fine china! The cost of employing tea ladies to deliver, collect and wash up, and of laundering the lace, is far from negligible.

Management's responsibility is to provide every employee from top to bottom with a drinkable beverage in a civilised form of container.

One afternoon, a consultant working at Budgerigars found himself in a particular department discussing the details of a system when the tea trolley came round. He was extremely dry and looking forward to a cup of tea. The tea lady carefully issued a cup of tea to each clerk, served in rather chipped, thick china cups which had clearly seen better days; but she wheeled her trolley away without serving a cup for the consultant. When he pursued her and asked for a cup of tea she explained that, as a senior executive, he was entitled to a senior executive's cup of nice thin bone china with a gold rim — and regrettably she had none on her trolley so could not serve him! Eventually she was persuaded to give him one of the chipped thick cups that were apparently good enough only for the 'ordinary' staff. In this particular company the management was subsequently prevailed upon to stop this nonsense, which only caused bad feeling. Obviously, some kind of compromise between thick chipped china ware and bone china cups with a real gold rim was necessary!

The fast-ring phone

Some years ago manufacturers introduced on to the market a form of internal telephone system whereby a manager telephoning a subordinate could make the phone ring at twice the normal speed — presumably to indicate to the subordinate that the boss was calling and should be answered in double quick time! Naturally, the effect of the double ring is to irritate the subordinate, who often finds that the subject matter of the call is of no great consequence anyway!

TV set

From time to time one meets the executive who feels that he must have a TV set in his office. Now that Prestel and similar services are available we can expect this demand to be on the increase.

> A public relations executive at Shovelup Corp. insisted that he should have a TV set installed in his office for his personal use. He pointed out that this was a commercial necessity since, by the nature of his job, he had to keep an eye on competitive advertisements and the like.
>
> In due course his TV set was installed and for a couple of afternoons he amused himself watching the racing and in between whiles looking at the advertisements.
>
> In the fullness of time the maintenance supervisor was instructed to remove a vital part from the set. After three months without any comment at all from the executive the TV set was removed; but of course by then Shovelup's had already wasted a lot of money.

Managers should beware of demanding toys of this nature and, in particular, unnecessary visual display units either linked to their own computer or to one of the public information services which are now blossoming. Such things are extremely useful if really required but nothing more than a sop to vanity if they are merely for amusement or to impress.

Essential reading

It is important for managers to keep up to date with developments and events in the areas of business in which they are interested. However, it is not unknown for this to be extended to an absurd degree.

This is illustrated by the executive who insisted that amongst his essential reading were three daily newspapers and copies of several magazines. The magazines included *Punch, Country Life, The Field* and sundry motoring magazines. He justified this collection on the basis that it was important for him to check whether the company's competitors were advertising in these particular journals. Of course, his real objective was to obtain the magazines he wanted to read free of charge.

Apart from the waste of money, his secretary and subordinates had formed the conclusion that he spent most of his time in the office reading the magazines rather than doing the job. This did nothing to enhance his reputation or to encourage any respect for him as a manager.

The executive loo

There is a breed of management executive which adopts the attitude that some form of elite treatment is due to them.

The chairman of a meeting at Coracle International's head office decided after a couple of hours that there should be a short break. Everyone trooped from the room and most of the men headed straight for a door just down the corridor marked 'Gentlemen'. Two senior executives set off in the opposite direction and called a third man to join them, explaining that they were on their way to the senior managers' loo on the next floor up. Intrigued to discover what made the senior managers' loo so special that it was worth the trouble of climbing a flight of stairs for, the third man decided to accompany them. The executive loo turned out to be a rather smart establishment where hairbrushes, combs and sundry aftershaves were provided free of charge.

A subsequent vist by the third man to the 'ordinary' loo found that it was essentially the same — that is, the porcelain was no different — but there was a singular absence of aftershave lotion, and more risk of getting into conversation with the lesser mortals.

While on the subject of executive loos, it is of interest to record a real-life incident involving the finance director of a large company.

One morning, clearly in a state of considerable agitation, the finance director of Scrouch and Company Plc summoned an administration executive to his office, indicating that the matter was of the utmost importance. The young executive arrived to find the director almost purple with rage. It transpired that in the executive loo on the executive floor of the building there was a hair cream dispenser, but on that particular morning he had found it empty. At first the bemused young executive thought he was the victim of some kind of practical joke: surely no one in such a position would get so worked up over a trivial matter like an empty hair cream dispenser!

However, it turned out to be a Serious Matter. The tragic news was passed to the appropriate member of the administrative staff who in turn administered a mild rebuke to the maintenance man for failing to carry out the vitally important function of topping up! Although nothing was said to anyone else about the incident, the story soon went round the office and the director in question earned himself the title 'The Brylcream Kid'.

The Personal Assistant

Managers should beware of employing a Personal Assistant (not to be construed as Executive Secretary). Although there are occasions when a promising executive is made P.A. to a senior man as part of a planned career development, in order to give him exposure and experience in a particular aspect of business, the appointment of such a body is usually little more than an advanced form of status symbol.

Such an appointment can create problems for senior management staff. For instance, if the boss's P.A. goes to a senior manager with instructions from the boss, the senior man may be inclined to disregard them, feeling that if the boss needed to give instructions he would wish to discuss the subject concerned; and in any case the senior manager could have no means of knowing whether or not the instructions as given were the ones actually intended.

Personal assistants are open to two temptations. One is to become merely a messenger boy — a sort of mobile filing clerk serving no really useful purpose; and the other is to assume the mantle of authority vested in the boss. The latter type especially can be an annoying time-waster.

> The area manager's personal assistant arrived at one of Squirt Hosepipes' branch offices and, using the authority of his boss, called a meeting of all the heads of departments. He proceeded to lay down the law on certain aspects of the management of the branch and would listen to none of the objections raised. He then departed with a look of triumph and importance. Subsequently the most senior manager at the branch telephoned the P.A.'s boss for confirmation of the new instructions, only to find that the boss himself had no knowledge of them. The P.A. had dreamed up the whole thing himself and decided to adopt the appropriate executive role.

Committees

It has been stated that the problem with a committee is that jointly the members are unable to agree and individually they are not responsible!

One certain way of killing any good idea is to set up a committee to discuss it. Indeed, setting up a committee is often used as a technique to prevent an idea being taken any further! (See p. 59.)

If a job needs to be done, and it requires more than one person to do it, then the manager would be well advised to set up an action team comprising an acceptable *minimum* number of people and to provide these with a written objective and a time limit in which to achieve it. This puts the onus of responsibility and achievement on somebody's shoulders and there is then a reasonable chance of obtaining a result.

Secrecy

A manager at Banjax Batteries prepared a report on a very confidential subject and in accordance with the company rules had only one copy typed (there were no carbon copies or copies for the file). The report was given to a senior member of the company who locked it up in his desk. Some weeks later the writer of the report discovered that certain information in the report needed modification and he went to ask the senior man for permission to amend it. The man was not in his office and his secretary seemed doubtful indeed that this would be allowed because of the confidential nature of the material. The secretary later rang to confirm that her boss would under no circumstances allow anyone to see the report; he was amazed, she reported, that the manager even knew he had such a thing. Apparently he had completely forgotten who had written it in the first place!

Of course, this is merely an example of mental aberration, but there are numerous cases where secrecy is taken to absurd lengths. It is not uncommon to find an organisation where policies have been agreed and objectives laid down, but these have not been passed on to the people who are supposed to achieve them because they are regarded as confidential and should not be mentioned outside the conference room. Unnecessary secrecy hampers the activities of staff who are denied information essential to the proper performance of their jobs.

Managers may be afraid that if they pass on certain information one of their employees will blurt it out in the wrong place and perhaps, for example, competitors will hear something that the company would not wish them to hear. This is a misunderstanding of human nature. If an employee is told that material is secret and confidential and he is being trusted with it, then he will almost invariably rise to the occasion. Of course, he *may* be unscrupulous and he *may* sell confidential information elsewhere. But in this unlikely circumstance, even if you do not pass on the information, he will find it out by other means.

The abuse of Organisation and Method services

Some companies have a healthy and active organisation and methods department which, if properly managed, provides a great deal of assistance to the company as a whole and the individual employees in it. Other managements, however, make a fundamental mistake of regarding their O & M department as a sort of 'hit squad' whose job it is generally to carry out fault-finding expeditions, even to the extent of going round with the axe! This is an abuse which the genuine O & M man will not accept and which the professional manager will not encourage.

It requires little intelligence to wander around a company looking for faults; and if a manager wants to get rid of some of his staff then he should show the courage of his convictions and do it himself.

The misuse of O & M services is invariably the action of an inadequate man who has hitherto mismanaged his function and lacks the integrity and intelligence to solve his own problems. Conversely, the intelligent manager wishing to improve his performance and that of his staff will use O & M services in a constructive and friendly way; a manager should take every opportunity to improve his performance including advice from qualified outsiders.

Wasting consultants' time — and company money

This is an advanced form — and a costly one — of the 'I know best' syndrome (see p. 85). Consultants frequently experience the problem of the company which, having employed them, refuses their advice. It is especially marked when advertising agents are employed. The agency, having carefully researched the market, categorised the product and its market segment, produces proposals to create a suitable image. It is at this point that the self-appointed expert (often the Chairman) moves in. He condemns all the proposals, and insists on an approach which he has taken 'straight off the top of his head'.

Now, if the Chairman knew all along what was wanted, why did the company call in the experts in the first place? The same treatment may be dealt to architects, film producers, script writers, office designers and computer systems analysts. It begs the question: what would occur on an operating table? Would the Chairman tell the surgeon which bit to cut next?

The interview show-off

Recruitment interviewing is a professional process which should be approached in a professional way, and anyone who has not been trained how to do it should obtain such training before launching into this particular aspect of the management role. Alas, there are many who do not bother . . .

> A 21-year-old employee was transferred to one department from another after she had been with the company for about three months. While discussing her experiences thus far in the company with her new manager she confided that she had been so upset at her initial interview that she had almost not accepted the job offer.
>
> Apparently, she had been given an appointment to see the personnel manager at 11 a.m. but on arrival she was asked to wait. The personnel manager showed up at noon and told her that he was an extremely busy man and it would be necessary for her to wait a little longer whilst he attended to other more urgent matters.
>
> She then waited until approximately 1.00 p.m. when the personnel manager reappeared and announced that he was now going for lunch but would be back very soon and would she please wait. She wondered whether she had time to get lunch herself, but was not very familiar with the district and wasn't sure whether there was a nearby sandwich bar or something else that was quick; and in any case she had no knowledge of how much time she had available to herself.
>
> She thus waited throughout lunch and finally, reaching a point of extreme discomfort, enquired from someone where she could find a ladies' lavatory. This matter had been neglected by the personnel manager.
>
> The personnel manager reappeared at about 2.30 in the afternoon and calling her into his office started the interview by asking her aggressively why she felt that she should be given a job by this particular company. She did her best to answer this question and was then asked what salary she wanted. She was embarrassed by this difficult question, it being her first job after leaving college. She gave her interviewer a figure and he jumped to his feet and shrieked, 'What makes you think you are worth that to us?'
>
> After this, apparently, the interview became rather more sensible and humane and eventually she was offered and accepted the job.
>
> Later this matter was taken up with the personnel manager who remembered the occasion well and said, 'I wanted to see what she was made of'.

This kind of approach, which claims to test the tenacity of an individual, is merely a form of showing off by the interviewer. It is not necessary to have someone with a rhinoceros-type hide to do the majority of jobs; and the chances are that this aggressive and rude treatment will deter many valuable people, who would otherwise have been happy to join the company.

Another type of interview show-off prefers to spend the interview time telling the job candidate about himself — what an important man he is and what an important job he does — and makes little effort to find out anything about the interviewee. Unfortunately, managers who find this an irresistible temptation are also prone to employ the candidate who seems most impressed by their bragging.

" . . . and so, as you can see, I am really a very important man."

Action check list

- [ ] Delegate!
- [ ] Don't insist on checking everything yourself.
- [ ] Don't be an obsessive collector of data.
- [ ] Don't let your secretary decide commercial priorities — directly or indirectly.
- [ ] Don't automatically promote the longest-serving employee on your payroll.
- [ ] Don't ignore talent already on your payroll.
- [ ] If you can't get a decision — act!
- [ ] Keep in touch with the shop floor.
- [ ] Beware of status symbols.
- [ ] Beware of using personal assistants.
- [ ] Be sparing in the use of committees.
- [ ] Avoid unnecessary secrecy.
- [ ] Use your O & M service constructively.
- [ ] Learn how to interview.
- [ ] Use consultants with care.

18

For the acquisition of sound managerial skills . . .

Having reached this point in the book the reader may be feeling that all is gloom and doom in management. This is certainly not so. There are probably as many good managers as bad — and there are companies with success stories to tell. Few managers are so bad or so perfect that they cannot improve their techniques by studying examples of good management and by making efforts to learn about management methods from the experts. If a manager — even a good one — does not keep himself well-informed, how can he train and develop his staff successfully?

. . . Study some model companies

Boots Ltd provide a first class example of how to communicate with employees. A few minutes can be very well spent in looking at one or two of their annual reports to staff. Here is a company which has realised how worthwhile it is to bring their employees into the picture and to provide them with information on such subjects as:

— Income and how it is spent.
— Developments, innovation and expansion.
— Future plans such as new products and markets.
— How many working days were lost due to sickness, etc.
— How many disabled people are employed.

Not only is this information satisfying to the curiosity of employees but it also helps prevent rumours and, very important, makes employees feel part of the company. In other words information such as 'how we are doing' is not limited to the board of directors and shareholders.

Telephone Rentals Limited also issue a house journal and a report to staff. Both are worth looking at although some may find the house journal rather 'stiff' in style.

Boots also do a good job in training their employees. This applies at all levels and does not exclude the part-time retail staff such as Saturday workers. These employees, mostly young and not seeking a career in the company, are, for example, provided with easy to read leaflets on the products they will sell *before* starting the job. This not only makes the employees feel more confident and relaxed but also encourages a better service to the customers. This action is a good example of how thoughtful treatment of staff can be a positive contribution to profits. Well served customers are more likely to come back than badly served customers.

Successful budgeting is a feature of the hotels division of *Trust Houses Forte*. Each hotel manager is actively involved in the forecasts of sales, costs, and the like for his unit of the business, and the process of analysis and estimating goes through area and regional levels of management. This means not only that all management levels are involved and become committed to the resulting targets, but also that a thorough re-think of many aspects of the business takes place each year.

The follow-up stage — reporting results each accounting period — again encourages active participation and repeatedly focuses attention on problems and opportunities.

National Westminster Bank concentrate a lot of skilled attention on induction of new employees and their subsequent development and training. This is an investment in the people — the main asset of a labour intensive business.

Marks & Spencer set new standards in reviewing and simplifying paperwork systems with their 'Good Housekeeping Drives'. These started in the 1950s and have been repeated from time to time. Challenging the need for various forms, records, etc. not only led to the elimination of costly paper but also the manpower costs associated with it. Above all M & S were challenging the necessity for whole procedures including 'controls' — no doubt at one time the beloved brain-children of bureaucrats.

Elimination of unnecessary paperwork with its drain on time raises the momentum of business, and aids achievement of the real objectives as opposed to spurious activities which do not contribute to profits.

Apart from the 'Good Housekeeping Drives' there is another key to the success of Marks & Spencer namely, the fostering of good human relations. The Chairman, Lord Sieff, summed up this aspect of management policy as follows:

> The development of good human relations in industry is very important. I use the term "good human relations in industry" rather than "industrial relations" because we are human beings at work, not industrial beings. Fostering good human relationships with customers, suppliers and employees means more than just paying good wages. Managers must be aware of and react to the problems of employees. Top management must know how good or bad employees' working conditions are. They must eat in the employees' restaurants, see whether the food is well-cooked, visit the washrooms and lavatories. If they are not good enough for those in charge they are not good enough for anyone.'

Much of this brings us back to where we started (see Chapter 1).

The point is that there are numerous successful companies to look at for actual 'how to do it' examples. The professional manager will make it part of his job to seek out and evaluate the methods and experience of other people.

. . . Consider some organised training

Throughout the book emphasis has been placed on the manager's need to ensure that *anyone* carrying out a management task has the necessary skills before starting out. Most managers are busy people and, although extended training is no bad thing, a few short courses are often more easy to arrange. The following reputable organisations all provide short courses and seminars.

Cranfield school of Management, Cranfield, Bedford, MK43 0AL. Tel: Bedford (0234) 751122. Telex: 826559.
> Cranfield provide a wide range of courses, normally of five days' duration. Courses on Corporate Planning and Management Techniques are particularly worthwhile.

British Institute of Management Foundation, Management House, Parker Street, London WC2B 5PT. Tel: (01) 405 3456.
> BIM offer one and two day seminars on such subjects as Time Management, Deciding Corporate Marketing Direction, Managing People and Office Automation. The main conference facilities are now at BIM, Management House, Cottingham Road, Corby, Northants WN17 1TT, where there is also a library of business books available to individual members and member companies.

The Industrial Society, Peter Runge House, 3 Carlton House Terrace, London SW1Y 5DG. Tel: (01) 839 4300.
> The Industrial Society courses, held in London and at a variety of regional centres, include subjects specifically designed for junior and middle and senior managers. Topics regularly covered are Industrial Relations, Leadership, Decision Taking and Delegation. Courses are also available on Word Processing, Telephone Selling, Secretarial Skills and Catering.

Keith London Associates, 40 Stonehills, Welwyn Garden City, Herts AL8 6PD. Tel: Welwyn Garden City (07073) 30114/5. Telex: 291807.
This company offers a range of computer courses.

Management Centre Europe, Avenue des Arts 4, B1040 Brussels, Belgium. Tel: (02) 219.03.90. Telex: 21.917.
Courses and conferences are normally conducted in English and include a wide range of management topics. MCE employ visiting speakers who are actively practising in the subject concerned, and the courses offer a good opportunity to 'pick the brains' of an expert aware of the realities of business.

. . . Use films as a training aid

Another source of valuable know-how is films. A good film on a management topic is easy to assimilate, takes up only a small amount of time and is relatively cheap. One of the leading suppliers is:

Video Arts, Dumbarton House, 68 Oxford Street, London W1N 9LA. Tel: (01) 637 7288.

Films on Finance, Interviewing, Communications, Sales techniques etc. can be purchased or hired and provide an entertaining and painless way to cover the subject. The films (16mm colour with optical sound, or on video cassette) are backed up by easy-to-read booklets which give the 'guts' of the subject.

Groups of managers will find it profitable to spend, say, 20 minutes watching the film and then perhaps a further 30 minutes discussing the subject in the context of their own business.

Video Arts films are available in America from the following sources.
East Coast: *Video Arts Film Productions, RFD Number One, Sterling Forest, Tuxedo, NY 10987. Tel: (914) 351 4735.*
West Coast: *Visucom Productions Inc, PO Box 5472, Redwood City, Calif. 94063. Tel: (415) 364 5566.*

. . . Read relevant and useful books

Planning a reading programme can be a problem to busy managers and there are so many books available that it is often difficult to know where to start.

A good (and inexpensive) introduction to a range of subjects can be found in the 'Notes for Managers' series published by the Industrial Society. These booklets cover the fundamentals of a subject in about 20 pages. In other words they can be read on a short train journey! Titles in the series include the following:

The manager as a leader; The manager's reponsibility for communication; Training your staff; Effective supervision in a factory; Effective supervision in the office; A guide to employment practices; A practical guide to joint consultation; The manager's guide to target setting; Industrial relations; The manager's responsibility for safety; Absenteeism — causes and control; The manager's guide to the behavioural sciences; Salary management; Appraisal and appraisal interviewing; Delegation; Induction; Management training by the Do-It-Yourself system; White-collar unions; Selection interviewing; Effective team building; Chairmanship and discussion leading; Effective discipline; Supervisors, their selection, training and development; Decision-taking; The manager's responsibilities for health; Effective use of time; The manager's responsibility for the development of employees.

Another concise source of information is provided by the British Institute of Management publications 'Management Checklists'. These 4-page leaflets provide a brief introduction, a reading list and a number of questions to start the manager thinking. Subjects covered include:

Effective use of executive time; Manpower planning; Induction; Selecting staff; Planning a meeting; Decision-making; House journals; How effective are your older managers? Controlling labour costs; Are you delegating?

Rather more meaty but still quick to read are the BIM Management Survey reports covering a range of subjects from Business Cars to Incentive pay schemes. These provide information on what other companies do; this of course may not necessarily be right for your company, but other people's methods can provide ideas.

For the manager who is prepared to put in more time the following titles are recommended:

John W. Humble *Improving business results* Pan Books Ltd.
This book provides a number of ideas on analysing your position and setting objectives.

Frank Finch *A concise encyclopedia of management techniques* Heinemann.
Some readers will find parts of this book hard going but there is no better way of finding out quickly what techniques are available and their applications.

R. L. Boot, A. G. Cowling, M. J. K. Stanworth *Behavioural sciences for managers* Edward Arnold.
The human side of things is explained in this title, which helps managers to appreciate what makes employees tick.

Antony Jay *Management and Machiavelli* Hodder & Stoughton Ltd.
This title is probably more entertaining if Machiavelli's *The Prince* is read first. However, this is not essential as the book stands alone as a thought-provoking examination of company politics, organisation, management style, and so on.

The author sincerely hopes that managers and potential managers have found the information presented in this book helpful. There is one more factor which every manager needs to be successful — good luck.

GOOD LUCK!

Notes

Notes

A selection of bestsellers from Sphere

FICTION

THE GREAT ALONE	Janet Dailey	£3.99 ☐
THE PANIC OF '89	Paul Erdman	£2.99 ☐
WHITE SUN, RED STAR	Robert Elegant	£3.50 ☐
A TASTE FOR DEATH	P. D. James	£3.50 ☐
THE PRINCESS OF POOR STREET	Emma Blair	£2.99 ☐

FILM AND TV TIE-IN

BLACK FOREST CLINIC	Peter Heim	£2.99 ☐
INTIMATE CONTACT	Jacqueline Osborne	£2.50 ☐
BEST OF BRITISH	Maurice Sellar	£8.95 ☐
SEX WITH PAULA YATES	Paula Yates	£2.95 ☐
RAW DEAL	Walter Wager	£2.50 ☐

NON-FICTION

TREVOR HOWARD: A GENTLEMAN AND A PLAYER	Vivienne Knight	£3.50 ☐
INVISIBLE ARMIES	Stephen Segaller	£4.99 ☐
ALEX THROUGH THE LOOKING GLASS	Alex Higgins with Tony Francis	£2.99 ☐
NEXT TO A LETTER FROM HOME: THE GLENN MILLER STORY	Geoffrey Butcher	£4.99 ☐
AS TIME GOES BY: THE LIFE OF INGRID BERGMAN	Laurence Leamer	£3.95 ☐

All Sphere books are available at your local bookshop or newsagent, or can be ordered direct from the publisher. Just tick the titles you want and fill in the form below.

Name _____

Address _____

_____

Write to Sphere Books, Cash Sales Department, P.O. Box 11, Falmouth, Cornwall TR10 9EN

Please enclose a cheque or postal order to the value of the cover price plus:

UK: 60p for the first book, 25p for the second book and 15p for each additional book ordered to a maximum charge of £1.90.

OVERSEAS & EIRE: £1.25 for the first book, 75p for the second book and 28p for each subsequent title ordered.

BFPO: 60p for the first book, 25p for the second book plus 15p per copy for the next 7 books, thereafter 9p per book.

Sphere Books reserve the right to show new retail prices on covers which may differ from those previously advertised in the text elsewhere, and to increase postal rates in accordance with the P.O.